Design and Plant
a Mixed Border

Design and Plant
a Mixed Border

Noël Kingsbury

WARD LOCK

A WARD LOCK BOOK

First published in the UK 1997
by Ward Lock
Wellington House
125 Strand
London
WC2R 0BB

A Cassell Imprint

Distributed in the United States
by Sterling Publishing Co., Inc.
387 Park Avenue South, New York, NY 10016–8810

Distributed in Canada
by Cavendish Books Inc.
Unit 5, 801 West 1st Street
North Vancouver, British Columbia
Canada V7P 1PH

A British Library Cataloguing in Publication Data block for this
book may be obtained from the British Library

ISBN 0 7063 7367 7

Designed by Roger Daniels
Illustrations by Wendy Bramall, Wayne Ford and Robin Carter
Printed and bound in Hong Kong by Dah Hua

CONTENTS

Introduction

A MIXED BORDER is one in which shrubs, roses, perennials and annuals are grown together, and such borders are at the heart of today's ornamental garden, for they extend the season of beauty and interest for as long as possible. Designing and planting a mixed border is all about interweaving plants to get the best value out of the available planting area. Public parks and grand gardens can afford brilliant displays of bedding or banks of flowering shrubs or even the traditional summer herbaceous border, but most of us work on a smaller scale and have to make the most of a limited garden.

The dictionary defines a border as an edge, boundary or frontier, reminding us of the origins of garden borders. As lawns became a popular feature of gardens in the nineteenth century, so planting tended to become restricted to a strip along the outside of the garden, and thus usually with a backdrop in the form of a fence, hedge or wall. It was not long before the border became an end in itself, a special category of garden art, and the lawn (and sometimes the rest of the garden) became mere foreground. The border went from strength to strength, so that by the time of the First World War, the border had become the chief ornament of many a garden and the source of the gardener's greatest pride.

Such borders relied almost entirely on summer-flowering herbaceous perennials, and they were labour intensive and thus beyond the reach of those who could not afford a staff of gardeners. The twentieth century saw a great rise in interest in 'cottage gardens', which were characterized by a more care-free planting of flowers, both annual and perennial, alongside vegetables and herbs, in emulation of the

A traditional herbaceous border in the grand manner.
A joy in late summer but hard work to maintain,
it is dominated by Michaelmas daisies (*Aster novi-belgii*
varieties) and white *Leucanthemella serotina*.
Plants in a border like this require annual feeding,
staking and, often, annual division.

plantings carried out by working-class country people. There was less emphasis on precision and order, leading garden designers like Vita Sackville-West to experiment with a more fluid (and lower maintenance) style and to work with a wider range of plants, including roses, other shrubs and annuals.

The cottage garden, which did not have a lawn (originally an upper class luxury), introduced gardeners to the idea of not planting in 'borders' as such but of planting in broad masses, with paths wending between. Dutch and German gardeners tend to adopt this approach anyway, the border as edge being a British concept. Nowadays, gardeners are more likely to consider not just having a mixed border in the traditional place, along a backdrop of some kind, but also 'island beds', which are free-standing plantings surrounded by lawn, or 'open borders', which have been inspired by colourful wildflower meadows.

Modern gardeners have to work within many constraints. Not only is the size of the plot itself frequently restricted, but they must also be aware of the responsibility they have to a wider world and, in particular,

of the effects that their favourite pursuit may have on it. The demands that gardens place on water resources is one aspect of gardening, for example, that is especially keenly felt and sometimes bitterly resented. Many gardeners, too, are aware of the important role that gardens can play in wildlife conservation, providing a home for insects, birds and other animals. Sometimes these may even be the main focus of interest, and the garden becomes a miniature nature reserve and a place to watch birds. For such gardeners, the mixed border is not only the best way to pack as much interest into a small space as possible but is also the best form of planting to encourage wildlife.

Mixed borders are an opportunity for us to appreciate the richness and diversity of the plant kingdom, the wide range of leaf shape, colour and texture, the seemingly endless variation in colour that flowers have to offer, the scent, not just of flowers but of foliage and bark, the beauty of autumn colour and berries, even in the depths of winter, and the many subtleties of form and shape.

In a small garden a mixed border provides space to grow a variety of plant forms.
Shrubs, including standard roses, perennials, such as *Campanula latifolia* var. *alba*, and
annuals grow together in harmony.

1

Types of Mixed Border

Traditional borders tended to be rectangular, following the lines of a wall or hedge, but modern ones are just about any shape you could imagine. The size and shape of borders are among the first things that need to be considered when you are laying out a garden: they are where most planting is going to take place, and they can have a crucial effect on the rest of the garden. Borders are not just places to grow plants, however; they can help shape the whole garden — a border of tall, shrubby plants, for example, can be used to block off another part of the garden.

Strip Borders

The limitations of narrow, strip-like borders are self-evident, but such borders are often what gardeners' are stuck with in small, and especially in narrow, gardens. Narrow borders do have certain advantages, notably for those who garden their borders intensively and need to get access to the back of the planting without having to go into it. Annuals and bedding plants are obvious subjects for a narrow border since they need a fair amount of attention, and vegetables and herbs are even better suited to this kind of plot, for they need constant, ready access. Espalier-trained fruit trees or trained cane fruit, like blackberries or raspberries, are an especially effective and traditional use of a strip border if there is a fence or wall backdrop.

Good narrow planting looks ahead. Shrubs that can greatly exceed the border after a few years' growth are not wanted, although a little overgrowing of the boundary between border and lawn or border and paving or whatever can look good, helping to blur and soften boundaries. Erect plants are a great boon, allowing lower growing varieties to be grown around them, and climbers, too, are useful if there is a wall or fence to support them.

Since a narrow strip border has an obvious limitation — it is a bit like planting up a straight line — it helps to overcome this as much as possible by varying the height of the planting in the border; for example, taller shrubby plants can, every now and again, intersperse lower growing, more compact perennials and shrubs.

Island Beds

An island bed is a border that is free standing. There is a lawn or a hard surface around it, but there is no

Above: The colours of early autumn light up a narrow border, in which a honeysuckle and a small tree have been used to extend interest skywards. The yellow flowers are rudbeckia.
Right: If you have space, wide borders offer the greatest scope for planting. The heads of *Allium giganteum* poke through the pink achillea.

backdrop behind it and it is visible from all sides. Cut from the moorings of the backdrop, the island bed floats free. The basic idea is to have a core of larger plants, mainly shrubs and a few large perennials, with lower growing plants around the outside. The challenge to the gardener though, is that all the plants around the outside are visible at all times and there is, for example, less opportunity to hide bare stems behind other plants.

Breaking up areas of lawn with informally shaped island beds enables the plant-lover to grow a wide range of plants and to divide an expanse of garden into more interesting, discrete areas. The island beds can almost take over, as the lawn is transformed into paths that weave between bodies of border planting.

When you are planning island beds, you must think carefully about their proportions. A small island bed in a vast expanse of lawn always looks

Island beds free border planting from the constraints of a backdrop but require more skilful planting. Lupins and delphiniums bring colour to early summer among clumps of later flowering perennials.

Types of border

Many front gardens look like this, with a lawn in the centre and narrow strips of border around the edges, which do not offer much scope for good mixed planting.

The same garden but with one border made much wider so that it intrudes into part of the lawn and makes more space for a mixed border containing larger plants.

More of a gardener's garden, here the lawn is reduced to a small, central area surrounded by three good sized borders. There is room for several larger shrubs and lots of perennials.

overwhelmed. Large shrubs or trees can overbalance a small bed as well, rather like a cuckoo in a nest, especially if they begin to smother smaller plants.

Island beds are usually informal in shape, and as such they represent an excellent design solution for the gardener who does not feel confident about garden design, but there is no reason they should not be geometric, in which case careful positioning and, preferably, a symmetrical arrangement will look best to most eyes. The skill in laying them out is to do with the way that their shapes relate to their surroundings on the one hand and the plants in

them on the other. So, if you intend to grow particular plants, especially large ones, it is a good idea to plan their location in concert with laying out the border edges.

OPEN BORDERS

The open border takes the border yet another step further away from the traditional planting along a boundary. The open border is where an entire section of garden is planted with perennials and sometimes shrubs. This arrangement allows planting at the expense of lawn, a much more interesting

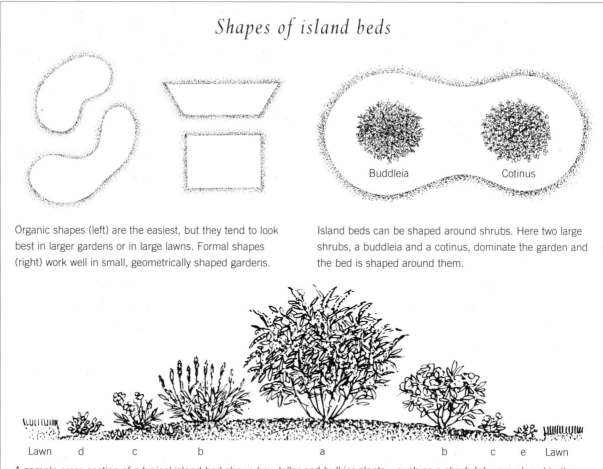

Shapes of island beds

Buddleia   Cotinus

Organic shapes (left) are the easiest, but they tend to look best in larger gardens or in large lawns. Formal shapes (right) work well in small, geometrically shaped gardens.

Island beds can be shaped around shrubs. Here two large shrubs, a buddleia and a cotinus, dominate the garden and the bed is shaped around them.

Lawn   d   c   b   a   b   c   e   Lawn

A sample cross-section of a typical island bed shows how taller and bulkier plants – such as a shrub (a) – are placed in the middle, with perennials (b) or smaller shrubs around them. Lower growing, bushy perennials or dwarf shrubs (c) are nearer the edges, which are occupied by very low perennials, annuals (d) or bulbs (e).

Grasses, perennials and annual bedding consort colourfully in an open border,
demonstrating vividly the scope that this contemporary style offers.

prospect for the true gardener, for whom maintaining grass is a chore, and the style is particularly suited to front gardens where the lawn tends to be largely ornamental rather than serving any useful function. Access is achieved from narrow paths that run across the area but that are practically invisible from more than a short distance away.

Traditional cottage gardens employ the open border concept, in that they do not have areas of lawn but are planted right across the garden area. The difference between gardens that are entirely planted with perennials or small shrubs – which is a type that is seen in front of many houses in the Netherlands – and the modern conception of the

open border is that the planting is an integrated whole. Particular distinctive plants or particular combinations of plants are repeated, so that the whole area is effectively tied together, and the resulting strong, visual impact is somewhat like that of a wildflower meadow.

The element of repetition is important to give the garden real impact, so having several plants of the more distinctive and reliable varieties scattered around is important. These 'theme plants' can make all the difference between a rather chaotic planting (which can still be attractive, in an artless, cottagey sort of way) and a really striking spectacle.

Open border plantings differ from conventional

borders or island beds in that there is no gradient of height, from tallest at the back to shortest at the front. Instead, there are carefully placed taller plants, which provide vertical interest throughout. These may be permanent, in the same way as shrubs, which are there all year round, or they may be seasonal, like tall grasses, such as miscanthus, or perennials, such as macleaya or hollyhocks. The open border type planting is usually quite low, with most of the plants below a height of 70cm/28in, so that, apart from a few taller plants, it is possible to see right across it. This low planting makes it especially suitable for gardens that are exposed to harsh, windy weather. It is possible,

however, to include a greater number of taller growing plants, which make the open border more like a wildflower meadow or prairie.

An increasingly popular version of the open border is the gravel garden. Here, plants are grown surrounded by gravel, which serves as an effective weed suppressant and helps to conserve moisture, as well as being a wonderful backdrop for a wide variety of plants. The overall character is of a dry, rather Mediterranean garden. Such a gravel garden is an especially attractive alternative to lawn and conventional borders in areas that experience regular summer drought.

Yellow achilleas, lupins, poppies and a variety of other perennials mingle in open borders, with narrow paths permitting access for maintenance and appreciation.

2

The Mixed Border in Garden Design

THE BORDER IS, for many gardeners, simply a place to grow plants, a place where they can enjoy their hobby, whether this is creating a carefully designed artistic spectacle or simply using the border as a convenient place to grow the plants to which they have taken a liking. But is the traditional border — the strip of planting running along a boundary or other backdrop — the best way for these plant-orientated gardeners to enjoy their interest? Island beds or open borders, where the lawn is replaced by wide swathes of planting, offer much more space to grow plants. If you do not need a lawn as a play area for children or as somewhere you can play games or entertain, consider getting rid of it or at least reducing it drastically in size. Lawns are dull compared with borders.

THE FUNCTION OF A BORDER

If a border is the main or, indeed, the only place you have to grow plants, it may have to perform functions that in an ideal world you would do elsewhere — a space for growing plants for cut flowers or even for fruit, vegetables and herbs. Such utilitarian functions need not detract from a well-planned border, and a recent trend in garden design is to make use of the decorative qualities of vegetables and herbs by integrating them into ornamental borders.

But borders have other purposes to perform, beyond being mere receptacles for planting, be it of an artistic or a botanical nature. They are not just canvases on which the artist paints pictures; they can also have a more important role to play. Consider the dictionary definition: borders are an ornament

Intimacy can be created by using borders to enclose and give special meaning to space. Hostas, green-flowered alchemilla and mauve *Geranium* × *magnificum* enhance the serene atmosphere.

to a boundary, a softening of the juncture between one place and another. It seems to be part of human nature that we like to blur boundaries, the place where a wall or fence meets the ground or where our property meets another's. Such situations are the traditional place for borders, and a mixed border, with its permanent framework of shrubs, is eminently suitable for this role, as there will be something there all year round. Such boundary borders can also be used as screening, to close off an unwelcome view, create privacy or separate areas of the garden from each other.

For many gardeners perhaps the most important role of a border is that it acts as a kind of backdrop for the garden as a whole. Backdrop is quite a pertinent word: theatre design and garden layout have been closely allied disciplines in many periods of history. Many of us regard the garden not just as a place where we enjoy gardening; it is also a stage. The garden is the immediate view from the house and the accompaniment to any use of the garden for social functions. Borders surrounding a lawn or patio that is used for entertaining can be more than 'living wallpaper', important though this is, they can play a more active role. Unusual plants, striking colour combinations, attractive scents – all these help to create a gently stimulating ambience and provide talking points.

Gardeners in urban environments will most probably be interested in using borders to help close their gardens off from the outside world or at least in providing a sense of separation from what the neighbours are doing. Those who live in the country may well think differently and want to feel that they are part of their surroundings, and here a border can perform a crucial role in blending the garden and the world beyond. Including a scattering of the wildflowers and shrub species that are occur naturally in the locality will help to relate the garden to its wider setting.

SHAPE AND SIZE

A look around the average suburb, the sort of place where people have gardens at both front and back, reveals that most front gardens conform to the same pattern: an area of lawn with a strip-like border going around it, hugging the wall, fence or hedge. Yet these lawns are often never used. It is on the back lawn that children play or barbecues are held. Those gardeners who love plants should look critically at this central place – in both spatial and metaphorical terms – that the lawn holds. Do you want to be a gardener or a groundsman? Consider digging it up, or at least a good part of it.

These conventional strip borders may be good for growing annuals, vegetables or flowers for cutting, for which constant attention, and therefore good access, is needed, but they severely cramp the style of anyone who wants to do anything more exciting. A border needs to be at least 2 metres/6 feet wide to grow any good-sized shrubs or roses or large perennials or to do any really creative design. In other words, if you want a genuinely mixed border it needs to be a decent width.

Cottage gardens and the nature-inspired plantings that are seen in continental Europe have made many gardeners realize that it is possible to do away with a lawn entirely and plant right across the

A long, narrow space is brought to life with a double border, which is made
strikingly effective by the repeat planting of silvery *Artemisia ludoviciana* and several other perennials.
Upright kniphofias echo the distinctive fencing.

Rethinking the borders in a small garden

There is a variety of possibilities, and you do not even have to move the path.

Four narrow borders around a lawn.

The border nearest the house has been extended to take advantage of the warm, sunny wall.

The borders at the front and one side have been extended, making room for some taller plants and thereby creating greater privacy.

If the borders around a small area of lawn were greatly extended, this could be very 'cottage garden' in style, with taller shrubs and perennials around the edges and lots of lower ones and annuals towards the centre.

In this fairly formal scheme, the borders around the edges have been made slightly wider and an island bed has been created in the centre.

The Dutch style is to get rid of the grass entirely and have an open border, with lower growing perennials and shrubs planted all the way across. The paths, of stepping stones or brick sunk into the soil, allow access to all areas.

Planning the shapes of borders and island beds

If the island bed, or indeed any border, is to include an existing tree, it is visually satisfying if the edge of the border either follows, or reflects, the outline of the tree canopy. This is a good idea in practical terms, too. Grass usually grows badly under trees, so replacing it with shade-tolerant ground cover usually works better. Even if the canopy of a tree or a large shrub in an island bed or border does not (or will not) reach the intended edge, having the edge bulge out as if to accommodate it creates a sense of harmony that links the shape with what it contains.

When you are laying out a border with a curving edge, use a hosepipe to mark the edge. It is easier to get a good curve with a hose than with string, and the hose will be more visible from a distance. Leave it in place for some time to get used to it and to see whether you still like it in a week's time. Ask your friends and neighbours for their opinions, too.

garden, so that the whole garden effectively becomes a border; this is the so-called open border.

Essentially, as we noted, border shapes fall into two categories: the geometrical, formal shapes, where straight lines rule, and the organic, free-flowing shapes, where all is curvy. Classical, formal gardens, which rely on symmetry, clipped hedges, geometrically shaped shrubs and tidy, ordered planting, are built up around a framework of straight lines and right angles. There is room for curves and other angles, but too many of these and the whole effect begins to fall apart. In a small garden it is probably best to keep to simple rectangular borders.

Informal gardens are more likely to use borders with curving edges, and it is possible to get a much more sympathetic relationship between the overall shape of the border and the plants in it this way. It is, for example, pleasing to have a bulge in the edge of a border to reflect the shape of a large shrub

or tree in the planting. It is also easier to 'get it right' with free-flowing shapes. There is a paradox, however: cottage garden-type planting or wild planting can look untidy in informal border shapes. One of the reasons why the twentieth-century English garden has been so successful is the balance that is maintained between formality and informality, between art and nature. Straight lines and a geometrical framework, supported by the occasional clipped shrub, look marvellous alongside burgeoning plant growth.

BACKDROPS

The borders of our gardening ancestors would have nearly always had a backdrop of some kind, with a gentle gradient from the tall plants at the back to the short ones at the front. This is still how most of us organize our borders, and there are good reasons why this is so. Most of us have only small gardens, and it makes sense to include a surrounding hedge,

ABOVE: Corn marigolds and scarlet mimulus mix with a purple agastache at the base of a wall.
RIGHT: *Macleaya cordata* and alstroemerias echo the colour of the brick in this
spacious midsummer planting.

wall or fence in the border design, usually partly obscuring it with our planting. Planting against a backdrop is also easy, because the resulting border is seen from one side only, which is a golden opportunity to hide the faults that many plants have — the lower halves of roses, with their gawky stems, can be hidden by lower growing plants.

A wall or fence as a backdrop has many functional purposes that can be turned to good ornamental advantage. It can be used to support climbers, for example, or weak-stemmed shrubs that need support as they grow or protection from severe weather, which is why the beautiful blue-flowered ceanothus is so often seen against walls. Hedges, though often attractive in their own right, offer few such opportunities. For one thing, planting is often not possible close to them because they withdraw moisture and nutrients from the soil; the Leyland cypress (× *Cupressocyparis leylandii*) is especially notorious in this regard.

A backdrop may be highly ornamental, like an old brick wall or a yew hedge, in which case it pays to consider carefully what colour scheme you are going to develop for the border that will front it. Pale colours and white look particularly good in front of dark yew, while warmer tones go well with brick. The colour of the brick or stone may be subtly picked out by choosing a similar shade for a dominant plant.

A fence is perhaps the least interesting backdrop, especially if it is of a kind that is mass-produced. Fences can be hidden, however, or put to good use supporting climbers. Taller shrubs at the rear of the border will do a good job either concealing it or breaking it up visually. Climbers will conceal the fence more rapidly and effectively though, and support wires for them may be easily fixed into the fence, although it should be borne in mind that climbers can get quite heavy over the years. Is your fence – or is it your neighbour's? – sturdy enough to take the weight?

If climbers are used extensively on a backdrop fence or hedge, they effectively become the visual backdrop. Evergreen climbers are few and far between – ivies (*Hedera* species) are the most common – but they do have the advantage that they are there all the year, providing continuity. Like ivies, *Parthenocissus* species (including Virginia creeper) remain relatively close to their supports, and thus neat and making a more or less uniform backdrop. Other climbers, such as roses, clematis and honeysuckles (*Lonicera* species), are less tidy and more likely to send forth branches in odd directions.

Finally, the height of the backdrop needs to be considered. Tall walls or fences may overshadow a border at their feet, but climbers will help to overcome this, serving to knit backdrop and border together. Low backdrops may easily disappear behind planting, especially if the border is wide in comparison to the height of the backdrop. If you feel that a backdrop is important, consider planting some tall shrubs at the rear to compensate.

SMALL SPACES

Small sites are always problematic, especially since there are often other problems that compound the limited space – soils filled with dry rubble and draughty spaces, for example – and that often seem hostile to any attempts at gardening. All too often in confined urban gardens there are few options in positioning a border: it has to go where the concrete stops or in the space between the path to the gate and the house wall. Where you do have some options you may well decide to base your decision on finding the best possible place for plant growth rather than on design considerations, and in these circumstances, your border will be in the only sunny corner, or in the only place that gets shelter from a cold wind or in the patch with decent soil.

If you have a choice, do not necessarily go for the conventional strip border. It may be fine for climbers, which can, of course, be important in small gardens, but growing plants in a line is extraordinarily uninteresting. It is often better to have a square border with a bit of depth than a series of two-dimensional lines of plants.

A small garden may have a larger area of fence and wall than of bare ground, making climbers, with their ability to soften and bring life to hard surfaces, vital. Climbers can green the city, bringing a touch

A dark hedge is a good backdrop for the lighter leaved foliage and pale colours
of *Alchemilla mollis*, lavender and *Yucca gloriosa*.

Cordylines are a source of evergreen architectural interest, which is particularly useful in small spaces. The white flowers are *Campanula persicifolia* var. *alba*.

of rural nostalgia and romanticism to urban life. They are a superb backdrop for other planting, and their screening abilities are often useful in densely populated areas.

When you are considering the planting of a border for a small space, bear in mind that foliage needs to play a much more important role than in a larger area. Flowers are a fleeting part of the natural world, a transient beauty compared to the more utilitarian value of leaves. Attractive evergreens will keep the garden interesting all year round, and even deciduous plants will provide a much longer season of interest than virtually all flowers. Plants that are chosen for their flowers should obviously have as long a season as possible,

and in small spaces it is probably more important to have one or two plants looking really good at any one time than it is to worry too much about the overall composition.

When foliage-based borders for small spaces are being planned, it is worth remembering that there are two good habitats for attractive evergreens: shade and hot, dry environments. Shade that is not too dry supports ferns, some of which are evergreen, hellebores, euphorbias and many other plants. Dry, sunny places are ideal for dwarf shrubs of the kind that thrive in a Mediterranean-type climate, nearly all of which are evergreen, including lavenders, sage (*Salvia officinalis*) and rue (*Ruta graveolens*). Both situations tend to occur around buildings.

3

Choosing a Site

MANY GARDENERS would probably regard being able to choose a site for a border as something of a luxury. All too often there is only one space suitable for any kind of planting, and the border and its plants have to be planned to fit. Often, too, the place for a border is more or less obvious in a garden with a wall or fence or some other kind of boundary that simply calls out for a border in front of it.

Those gardeners with more space can exercise more control over where a new border will go. Even so, some places are more obvious than others. But why do they seem obvious? The reason is probably that they are similar to situations in gardens we have visited or seen illustrated in books and magazines. Creative thinking, however, must challenge what at first sight seems obvious.

A fundamental conflict in siting a border is between visual effect and the prevailing conditions. One side of the garden may be crying out for a border – along a long, bare stretch of fence, for example – but the growing conditions may not be ideal because, perhaps, it is in shade. A border of shade-tolerant plants may be perfectly attractive, but it will not be as colourful as one in sun. Is this what you really want? If you passionately want to grow marigolds, lupins and lavender, perhaps you should think about creating an open border or island bed on the sunny side, leaving only a narrow border along the fence.

Before any such decisions are made, however, you need to be clear in your mind about what is most important to you. Are you more concerned about the appearance of the garden as a whole or

---

Plants for shady gardens

(D = some tolerance of dry shade)

SHRUBS
Aucuba japonica (D)
Buxus sempervirens
Euonymus fortunei
Ilex × altaclerensis; I. aquifolium
Fatsia japonica
Osmanthus
Pachysandra terminalis
Ribes (light shade)
Rubus
Vinca (D)

PERENNIALS
Aquilegia alpina
Aruncus
Aster divaricatus; A. macrophyllus
Astilbe

Bergenia (D)
Brunnera
Cimicifuga
Corydalis
Dicentra
Epimedium (D)
Euphorbia robbiae (D)
Geranium endressii;
    G. macrorrhizum (D); G. × oxonianum
Helleborus; H. foetidus (D)
Hosta
Iris foetidissima (D)
Lamium
Polygonatum
Primula
Symphytum
Tellima (D)

GRASSES AND GRASS-LIKE PLANTS
Carex pendula (D)
Luzula (D)
Melica
Milium effusum

FERNS
Nearly all ferns, but only the following are suitable for dry shade:
Asplenium scolopendrium
Dryopteris filix-mas
Polystichum acrostichoides;
    P. setiferum

Leaves last longer than flowers, which makes them invaluable for small spaces.
Shade lovers, such as the fern *Polystichium setiferum* and the hosta *H. sieboldiana*, often
have particularly attractive foliage.

about the cultivation of favourite plants – that is, do you choose the plants to fit the design or do you fit the design around the plants?

Because different kinds of plant grow in different situations, it is useful to consider what you can grow in a mixed border in a range of conditions.

ASPECT
Sun or Shade?

Full sun supports the widest variety of plant life, and the mixed border is no exception. The great majority of garden shrubs and climbers and most herbaceous perennials do best in full sun. In addition, nearly all annuals and bedding plants need sun for most of the day. It is certainly the best place to create a genuinely mixed border that will provide interest throughout the year and give you the opportunity to use a wide variety of plants and develop all sorts of effects with colour, shape and form.

Gardeners often tend to assume that the sun is necessarily desirable and treat shade as something inherently undesirable or problematic. This may

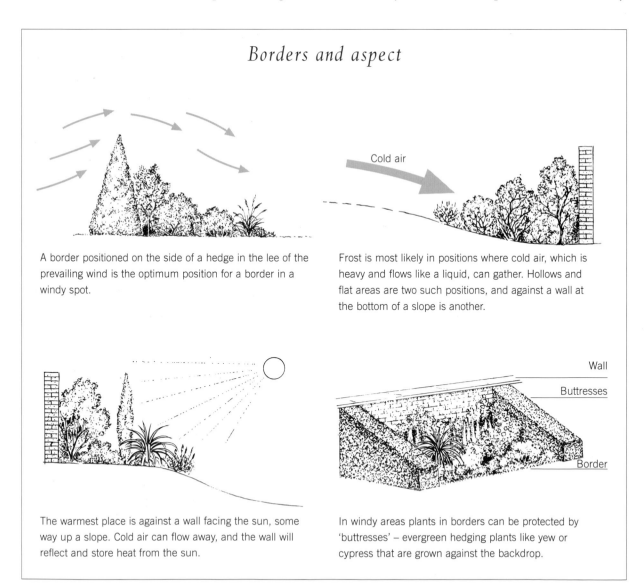

Borders and aspect

A border positioned on the side of a hedge in the lee of the prevailing wind is the optimum position for a border in a windy spot.

Frost is most likely in positions where cold air, which is heavy and flows like a liquid, can gather. Hollows and flat areas are two such positions, and against a wall at the bottom of a slope is another.

Cold air

The warmest place is against a wall facing the sun, some way up a slope. Cold air can flow away, and the wall will reflect and store heat from the sun.

In windy areas plants in borders can be protected by 'buttresses' – evergreen hedging plants like yew or cypress that are grown against the backdrop.

Wall

Buttresses

Border

be true if you want to grow cabbages, but it is not if you want a mixed border. As long as the shade is not too deep or dry there is ample scope for creating a fine mixed border with shade-tolerant shrubs and perennials. Indeed, there are those who would argue that the softer light enables more subtle colours to be appreciated. In addition, there is the advantage that many shade-loving perennials have particularly attractive and evergreen foliage, including bamboos, hostas, ivies and ferns, to name but a few. The disadvantages are that most of the flowering takes place earlier in the year, leaving the garden looking a bit dull from midsummer to autumn, and that there are few climbers or annuals that will thrive in shade.

Shade-tolerant plants tend to be comparatively small. There are few shrubs that will flourish in full shade – although quite a lot will tolerate light shade – and few perennials and ferns grow to heights of more than 70cm/28in. While you can make a respectable mixed border in light shade, it can be difficult in full shade to find sufficient taller plants, although most bamboos are shade tolerant. A border in such a place may have to be much flatter than one in a sunnier site, with a greater number of low-growing plants and less overall height.

Wind, Frost and Shelter

We are often quickly aware if a garden has particularly good or bad aspect. Less obvious is whether a garden is in a 'frost hollow' – that is, whether it lies in a dip or on an extensive area of flat ground where frost occurs readily because the substantially heavier cold air has nowhere to flow away to.

What are called micro-climates can have a major effect on what will flourish in a garden. Where cold winter winds or hard frosts are prevalent, the choice of plants will not be limited but it will have to made carefully. The majority of perennials and many shrubs come from climates where conditions regularly exceed what we feel are exceptionally cold winters. But we must be aware of plants that are slightly tender and restrict their use. Evergreens are likely to suffer 'wind chill' in exposed places, as is anything that starts into growth or flower early in the year.

Open borders with a lot of grasses, which tend to be hardy and, if tall, windproof, lower growing perennials and small, compact shrubs can be effective and look especially good on a large scale. This type of border also tends to require little in the way of maintenance.

Strong maritime winds may not be pleasant but they are not cold. There are many attractive plants,

---

Plants for cold, exposed sites

SMALL TREES
Betula
Laburnum
Salix alba
Sorbus

SHRUBS
Amelanchier
Elaeagnus commutata
Philadelphus spp.
Rhododendron (smaller varieties)

Salix
Viburnum (many varieties)

DWARF SHRUBS
Calluna vulgaris
Erica carnea; E. tetralix
Pernettya

PERENNIALS
Any perennials and grasses that are not too tall to be battered by the wind

are suitable – just how much can be learned only by trial and error in individual gardens, although taller perennials that do not need staking (see page 154) will help. Most perennials and grasses are extremely hardy. Finding out the plants' countries of origin often gives a good idea of the conditions they will tolerate.

including evergreens such as hebes, that will thrive in blustery conditions even though they are not particularly cold hardy. In areas where strong winds are a problem, plants need to be physically resilient: tall perennials like delphiniums are not suitable.

A sheltered garden offers all sorts of exciting possibilities for the mixed border. There is the chance to grow a much wider variety of plants than normal, and many somewhat tender plants are at their best in autumn, so if frosts are late, the border can look wonderfully colourful until late in the season. Many plants with dramatic foliage are tender – palms and cannas to name but two – so a mixed border in shelter can be a much more exotic affair than in an 'average' garden.

A border for such a planting really ought to take advantage of the special conditions that shelter it, and a gardener in such conditions should consider having a good wide bed at the foot of a sunny wall to take as many plants as possible. Not only do many tender plants, like abutilons and bottle brush (*Callistemon* species), grow fast, but collecting and experimenting with them is addictive.

SOIL CONDITIONS
Fertile or Infertile?

Deep and fertile soils reward the gardener rapidly and effusively. Roses and big showy perennials grow especially well in this kind of soil, and annuals and bedding thrive.

A huge range of plants – shrubs, perennials, annuals – will give you endless creative scope for interesting planting at practically all times of year. If there is room, consider a 'big' border, not just one that is wide but one that is full of large, exuberant plants that relish fertile soil. This border could include a few shrubs, including shrub roses, and large, late-flowering perennials, such as many

---

Plants for coastal areas

Plants with grey or silver foliage or tough, leathery foliage or with small,
needle- or scale-like leaves are usually good for coastal locations

SMALL TREES
Arbutus spp.
Eucalyptus spp. (if periodically cut
  back)
Sorbus

SHRUBS
Choisya
Cytisus
Elaeagnus
Euonymus fortunei; E. japonicus
Fuchsia magellanica
Ilex
Lavatera
Olearia
Phormium tenax

Pyracantha
Rosmarinus officinalis
Tamarix
Viburnum tinus
Yucca

DWARF SHRUBS
Erica
Hebe
Lavandula
Phlomis
Santolina

PERENNIALS
Achillea
Agapanthus

Artemesia
Aster (shorter varieties)
Bergenia
Eryngium
Euphorbia
Geranium
Iris
Kniphofia
Perovskia
Salvia (shorter varieties)
Sedum
Stachys

**GRASSES AND GRASS-LIKE
PLANTS**
Nearly all, except perhaps the tallest

Moist soils offer scope for lush planting. *Iris sibirica* and candelabra primulas, which flower
in early summer, thrive in such conditions.

members of the daisy family. Climbers will flourish here, too, whether climbing on the backdrop or free standing on supports.

Infertile soils are usually light and thin. They lose moisture and nutrients quickly, so making a stressful environment. Plants such as roses may grow but they will not grow well. The gardener is faced either with trying to improve the soil, which can prove expensive and labour intensive, or with concentrating on those plants that will do well. Many low-growing shrubs from harsh environments in nature, like lavenders, cistus and sage, will flourish, as will many of the ornamental grasses and a fair number of perennials. Most of

these flower in early summer, but many are evergreen, and maintaining year-round interest is not a problem.

Although some medium-sized and large shrubs will flourish, most of the plants for poorer soils are relatively low growing, rarely over 1 metre/3 feet high. There are certainly enough plants of various heights to make an attractive conventional border, but these kinds of plant look best in a relatively low, flat planting in island beds or open borders. Most look wonderful with gravel, which is appropriate given that many are from dry, stony environments. Lawn grass does not do well on poor or dry soils, and this is all the more reason to go for gravel.

Moist or Dry?

Plants that thrive on damp ground really show it. They tend to be big and luxuriant, growing vigorously and often with dramatic foliage, and there is a definite tendency to late-summer flowering. The sheer exuberance of many of these plants is a good reason to aim for as large a border as possible to provide plenty of space for large perennials to be seen at their best.

Perennials and grasses will provide most of the interest in a border on such a soil, with foliage being arguably as important as flower. Some shrubs and bulbs will thrive, too, providing winter and spring interest, but it will really be the perennials that dominate the scheme.

In dry soils plants tend to be small, compact and wiry, but by no means unattractive. In fact, many have evergreen grey foliage and particularly intensely coloured flowers. Most of what was said for infertile soils applies to dry ones as well, and the two are frequently linked.

Clays and Acid Soils

The problem with clay is not so much what the plants think of it as what the gardener thinks. It may be horrendous to work, but its fertility means that a lot of plants love it. Roses do especially well on clay, as do many of the larger late-flowering perennials. A lush border full of classic summer flowers should be the aim, but that involves working the soil as little as possible. Concentrate on perennials that can be left undisturbed for years on end and that do not need frequent dividing, such as Michaelmas daisies (*Aster novi-belgii* varieties) or phlox. Seeds do not germinate well in clay, so hardy annuals and bedding plants may be hard work.

Acid soils, which are often but not always also

Plants for soils liable to summer drought

SMALL TREES
Betula
Ilex

SHRUBS
Berberis
Brachyglottis
Buddleia
Ceanothus
Cistus
Cytisus
Genista
Lavatera
Ribes
Rubus

Tamarix
Yucca

DWARF SHRUBS
Artemesia
Ballota
Convolvulus cneorum
Hebe
Helianthemum
Lavandula
Perovskia
Phlomis
Potentilla
Santolina

Plants for moist, occasionally waterlogged soils

SMALL TREES		
Salix	Sorbaria	Ligularia
Sorbus aucuparia	Spiraea × vanhouttei	Lobelia
	Viburnum opulus	Lythrum
		Monarda
SHRUBS	**PERENNIALS**	Persicaria (some varieties)
Amelanchier	Aruncus	Primula
Clethra	Astilbe	Rheum
Cornus alba; C. stolonifera	Hosta	Rodgersia
Sambucus	Iris sibirica (and many others)	Trollius

Plants for thin, alkaline soils

SMALL TREES
Cercis siliquastrum
Malus
Sorbus (many varieties)

SHRUBS
Berberis
Buddleia
Buxus sempervirens
Caryopteris
Ceanothus
Cistus
Daphne mezereum
Deutzia
Euonymus
Forsythia

Fuchsia
Genista
Hebe
Philadelphus
Spiraea
Vinca
Weigela
Yucca

PERENNIALS
Achillea
Anaphalis
Aster amellus
Campanula persicifolia
Dictamnus
Digitalis (not *D. purpurea*)

Geranium psilostemon;
    G. sanguineum
Gypsophila
Iris germanica (bearded iris)
Nepeta
Polygonatum (in shade)
Salvia nemorosa; S. × superba
Sedum telephium

GRASSES AND GRASS-LIKE PLANTS
Elymus
Helictotrichon sempervirens
Pennisetum
Stipa

Poor, acid soils offer the opportunity to grow lots of colourful early-summer-flowering shrubs such as rhododendrons and azaleas. The bulb *Allium giganteum* provides a contrast in shape.

sandy, are poor in nutrients, and traditional border roses, perennials and annuals will not do well. However, nature has given us a remarkably colourful flora for these soils — rhododendrons, azaleas and heathers — along with many other less well-known, acid-tolerant shrubs. Acid soils on sheltered sites will support the larger rhododendrons and other shrubs, most of which are naturally woodland plants, as well as many woodland shade-loving perennials. In open conditions shrubs will dominate, because only a handful of sun-loving perennials will grow on these soils. Many acid-tolerant shrubs are quite small, so there is no shortage of attractive plants for the front of the border, and in shady conditions, shrubs can be mixed with woodland perennials, which gives particularly good scope for extensive low plantings of spring-flowering woodlanders.

The combination of an open, exposed situation and acid soil creates a hostile environment, but gardeners on such land are fortunate that the limited flora that does flourish there is often colourful and is nearly all evergreen. Taller shrubby species may not survive, except with shelter, so the emphasis must be on low, open borders or island beds.

Heathers, which seem to have a variety flowering for every month of the year, are the mainstay of such a planting scheme, along with the rather over-used dwarf conifers. More creative gardeners should consider the many grasses and sedges available to intersperse among the heathers.

SLOPES

In view of the fact that most gardens are not flat, it is surprising that so little attention is given to making borders on them. All too often they are put down to lawn to make a grassy bank or covered in boring evergreen shrubs. It is difficult to maintain a planting on a slope, of course, which means that any planting will have to be able to look after itself as much as possible. On steep slopes, where soil erosion is a possibility, good year-round ground coverage will be vital.

In spite of these problems, slopes offer exciting possibilities. Think of being able to look up at plants tiered one above the other, or having plants tumbling down, or using climbers as trailers and ground cover. Perennials with large foliage or with stems that arch outwards are particularly dramatic when planted on slopes.

Plants for acid soils

SMALL TREES
Acer palmatum
Betula
Enkianthus
Sorbus

SHRUBS
Berberis
Camellia
Cistus
Clethra
Fothergilla

Genista
Hamamelis
Kalmia
Pieris
Rhododendron

DWARF SHRUBS
Calluna vulgaris
Erica
Genista (small varieties)
Pernettya

PERENNIALS
Few perennials or grasses relish acid soils, but most will grow with reduced growth

GRASSES AND GRASS-LIKE PLANTS
Deschampsia
Festuca
Luzula
Molinia

4

Planning and Planting

*I*MPULSE BUYING affects gardeners as much as it does anyone else, and garden centres are as good as any other business at positioning their products so that we cannot but fail to notice them on our way to the check-out. While impulse buys in most other shops can be given away or even sold second hand if they do not seem so desirable in the cold light of day, the same is not true of plants, which have a tendency to get bigger and harder to move, or remove, with every day that they grow. Buying plants should be done with caution. Not only do you need to think carefully about how every plant you acquire is going to fit into the garden, especially if it is for the border, when it will have to look good alongside others, but also because it may well not thrive in the conditions of your garden.

CHOOSING PLANTS TO SUIT THE SITE

In the last chapter we saw how different types of soil and different aspects affected what sort of plants do well and the relevance of this for planning mixed borders. Acid soils, for example, support a wide range of shrubs but few perennials, which means that a border on such a soil will have to rely more heavily on woody plants and thus on a more permanent year-round structure than one that is based primarily on herbaceous perennials, which die down in winter.

Traditionally, gardeners have worked hard at changing the conditions in their gardens to suit the kind of plants that they want to grow. Peat and acidity-promoting chemicals are added to alkaline soils to enable rhododendrons to grow, while lime, manure and fertilizers are laboriously dug into poor acid ground so that roses and perennials will flourish. This approach is trouble enough when only a few special plants are wanted, but it involves a huge amount of work, and often money, when it is applied to a whole border.

Are wholesale attempts to change garden conditions worth the effort and expense? Such attempts often do not work in the long or even medium term. Attempts to change soil chemistry are usually short lived, and unless whole truckloads of new soil are imported, clay and sandy soils often stubbornly resist being turned into the fine loam seen on television gardening programmes. Dry and waterlogged soils are often the way they are for reasons over which we have little control. Moreover, attempts drastically to modify soil often involve environmental costs: the destruction of wetlands to extract peat and falling water tables to take water are just two of the most widely publicized.

The fact is that nature has beautiful and garden-worthy plants for practically every condition that it has created. Acid sands are the perfect soil for some of the most spectacular flowering shrubs, while waterlogged clay supports a lush and vibrant flora. If we work with nature when we plan garden borders we can save ourselves a lot of work and money, and reduce our impact on the wider environment, too.

So, when you are planning a garden border it is essential that you choose plants that will naturally thrive on the site rather than just choosing them on purely aesthetic grounds. Such a choice will ensure consistently good growth among all the plants of your mixed border. An ornamental rhubarb (*Rheum* species) may make a stunning contrast to a large lavender bush, but they will not necessarily be happy together. The wet soils that will make the rhubarb look its best may well prove to be too waterlogged for the health and even the survival of the lavender.

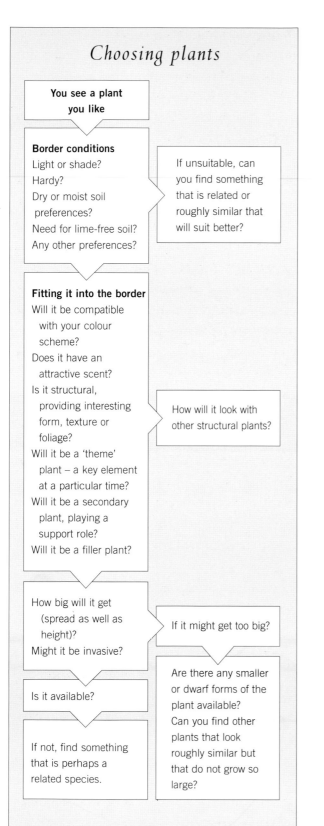

Choosing plants

You see a plant you like

Border conditions
Light or shade?
Hardy?
Dry or moist soil preferences?
Need for lime-free soil?
Any other preferences?

If unsuitable, can you find something that is related or roughly similar that will suit better?

Fitting it into the border
Will it be compatible with your colour scheme?
Does it have an attractive scent?
Is it structural, providing interesting form, texture or foliage?
Will it be a 'theme' plant – a key element at a particular time?
Will it be a secondary plant, playing a support role?
Will it be a filler plant?

How will it look with other structural plants?

How big will it get (spread as well as height)?
Might it be invasive?

If it might get too big?

Is it available?

Are there any smaller or dwarf forms of the plant available?
Can you find other plants that look roughly similar but that do not grow so large?

If not, find something that is perhaps a related species.

THEME PLANTS AND SUPPORTING PLANTS

'I don't know where to start,' is the commonly heard cry when garden owners are starting to plan a new border. It is all too easy to end up with a collection of plants that have been chosen individually, that do not relate to each other and that, when all planted together, look a disparate jumble. The choice of plants available is bewildering to the new gardener, although plant connoisseurs hold the opposite view: that there are many good garden plants that are difficult to get hold of.

The concept of 'theme plants' is a useful one, because it helps us not only to develop satisfyingly organized planting but also to organize our thoughts. The idea is that, in any border larger than the tiniest, one or more plant varieties are chosen to dominate, either all year round or for a particular period. They set the theme for the planting, and everything else has to play either a supporting role or a neutral one. One large plant can be used as a theme plant for a border or, if smaller perennials or annuals are used, several can be dotted around, serving to bring the whole border together.

The best theme plants are those that have quite a strong character, either of colour or shape, and that tend to stand out anyway. As we shall see, it is possible to use more subtle varieties as theme plants, but they have to make up for their lack of impact by being more numerous. The choice of theme plants must be practical. They must be hardy and reliable. It is no good building a planting around things that are going to die in the next hard winter or be scorched in the next hot summer. In addition, most of us will want them to establish quite quickly.

'Secondary plants' are those that are chosen to support and complement the theme plants, usually because the colour of their flowers or leaves looks good with that of the theme plants. If you are also paying attention to foliage and form, they may be chosen because their shape or the texture of their leaves fills a similar complementary role. Needless to say, secondary plants have less impact than theme plants. If really striking varieties are chosen they may compete with the theme plants, making the border too vivid or overwhelming in terms of colour or too fussy and restless in terms of foliage shape.

'Filler plants' are those that have less visual impact but are necessary to fill gaps and provide background. At the least they must look good with the theme and secondary plants, but they are often relatively neutral. Low-growing ground-cover varieties are particularly useful for filling gaps or awkward shady spots.

Shrubs as Theme Plants

Most shrubs are simply too large to have more than one example in a border, but their size and dominance when they are in flower make it necessary to consider them as theme plants. Many shrubs may be spectacular in flower but look dull and shapeless for the rest of the year, which makes it important that there is plenty of interest for the time that they are not in flower. Spring is the best time of year for flowering shrubs, and a well-placed flowering shrub or small tree can easily be a fine theme plant. Forsythia, for example, blooming bright yellow at the end of winter when we appreciate it most, may be an obvious theme plant. Yellow daffodils and tulips can be used to extend the colour throughout the border, with other bulbs providing contrasting colours.

Acanthus, which is distinctive and long lasting, makes a fine theme plant for summer.
The softness of fennel foliage makes it an effectively contrasting secondary plant.

Theme, secondary and filler plants

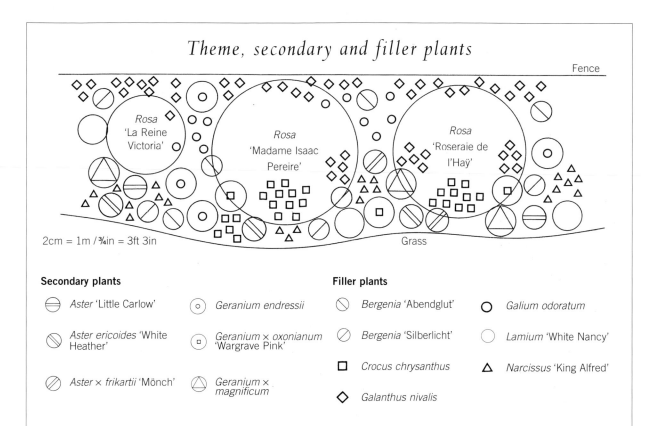

Fence

Rosa 'La Reine Victoria'

Rosa 'Madame Isaac Pereire'

Rosa 'Roseraie de l'Haÿ'

2cm = 1m / ¾in = 3ft 3in

Grass

Secondary plants

Aster 'Little Carlow'

Aster ericoides 'White Heather'

Aster × frikartii 'Mönch'

Geranium endressii

Geranium × oxonianum 'Wargrave Pink'

Geranium × magnificum

Filler plants

Bergenia 'Abendglut'

Bergenia 'Silberlicht'

Crocus chrysanthus

Galanthus nivalis

Galium odoratum

Lamium 'White Nancy'

Narcissus 'King Alfred'

The rise in popularity of the so-called old-fashioned and shrub roses, which have flowers in a myriad shades of pink, led to numerous borders being devoted largely to these plants. Rather than grow them in the traditional 'rose bed', an extremely labour-intensive and most unattractive way of gardening, they are now often grown in mixed borders. They are the theme plants, around which everything else revolves. Hardy geraniums are often grown with them as secondary plants because their colours – pinks and mauve-blues – complement the roses well and they fill out the space beneath and around them.

During late summer and autumn the roses will be well past their best, and some may even have finished flowering. Although some of the geraniums may still be flowering, another secondary plant is needed to keep the border interesting. Asters, including the well-known Michaelmas daisies (Aster novi-belgii varieties), are a good choice: they will make a colourful show for the end of the season and their colours – blues, purples, pinks and white – complement whatever roses are left.

There are various gaps left, however. Dark spaces or corners may be too shady for the geraniums to do well, so more shade-tolerant, ground-cover 'filler plants' are needed.

Galium odoratum is a good one, a white, spring-flowering perennial that dies down by the time the roses are making their maximum growth.

Winter may be a dull time, so bergenias are a good two-season, dual-purpose plant. They can be regarded as a theme plant for late winter and spring, with their attractive evergreen leaves and flowers in pinks (sometimes very bright) and white. Dead nettles (Lamium species) are useful, too: they are good for ground cover especially in shadier corners, they are evergreen, those with silver-variegated leaves often looking their best in winter, and they flower in spring. In summer, both bergenias and lamiums act as quiet filler plants.

With the addition of bulbs – crocuses, snowdrops and narcissi would be ideal – a whole new season of spring flowers may be created. Given their size and the relative strength of their colour it is useful to think of the narcissi as the theme plants for mid- to late spring, after the bergenias but before the roses.

All the plants mentioned do well on the same kind of soil – that is, on one that is averagely fertile and moist. The roses, geraniums and asters thrive on moister than average soils, and most kinds will also do well on heavy clay ones.

Repetition makes borders stand out. *Allium sphaerocephalon* and cornflowers
mingle with violas and the seedheads of *Allium christophii*.

Later in the year, however, the dull foliage and untidy habit of forsythia make it essential that other good theme plants take over and either hide it or draw attention away from it.

Some gardeners may like to use plant form rather than colour as the dominant element in a border. Architectural plants, like clipped yew and box, have an important role in many borders anyway (see page 81), but they can also be used to set the tone for classically formal plantings.

Choosing Theme Plants for Flower Colour

Using a strong colour for a theme plant will set the tone for the whole border, and using another strong colour might cause a clash. It also makes the choice of the other flower colours that will be out at the same time important. You cannot go far wrong with paler related colours — a magenta-flowered theme plant with pink-flowered secondary plants, for instance. More subtle colours can be used, but there should be plenty of them if they are to make an impact. Plants that can be propagated quickly and easily have an important role to play here. Small patches of hardy annuals that are easily sown as seed are one possibility, and perennials that readily sow themselves around are another. A good example of the latter are aquilegias, which self-sow throughout borders to create a mass of blue, purple and pink flowers in early summer.

Foliage Plants as Theme Plants

Foliage has the great advantage that it is around for much longer than flowers, an important consideration in a small space. This, and the fact that it is (nearly always) much more subtle than flower colour, makes foliage plants extremely useful as theme plants. A plant chosen for its attractive foliage may not dominate a planting in the way that beautiful flowers may do, but it will always be there in the background, running through the border, creating that all-important sense of continuity. The use of the dwarf grass, *Festuca glauca*, is a good example. When it is grown alongside heathers, hebes and other grasses that flourish in the windy environments they find congenial, it acts as a unifying thread.

INTRODUCING SCENT

For most people, colour is the most important factor in their gardens, and most want to have as long a season of colour as possible. As a consequence, borders are seen primarily as places to grow flowers. But there is far more to plant life than flowers, as more and more people are realizing. The shape of plants needs to be appreciated, along with their colour and the texture of their foliage, and then, of course, there is scent.

Scent is an elusive aspect of plants. It is difficult to remember precisely or to describe, and even more personal than preferences in flower colour. It is sadly underrated in commercial plant production, as scent-less modern roses illustrate, yet for many

Cotinus is one of the few shrubs that looks its best in late summer, thanks to the 'smoke' of its seedheads. Other seedheads contribute to the theme it sets.

Examples of theme, secondary and filler plants

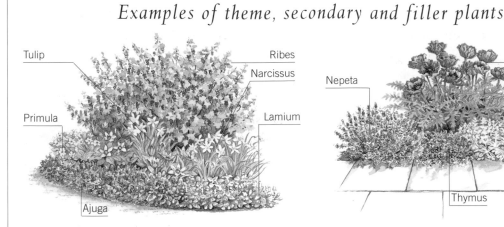

Tulip · Ribes · Narcissus · Primula · Lamium · Ajuga

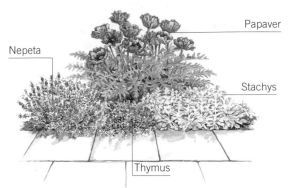

Nepeta · Papaver · Stachys · Thymus

In spring, with average soil conditions and a border in full sun or very light shade, the theme plant is *Ribes sanguineum* 'Pulborough Scarlet', the secondary plants are *Narcissus* 'Trousseau' and *Tulipa kaufmanniana* 'Ancilla', and the filler plants are *Lamium* 'White Nancy', *Primula vulgaris* and *Ajuga reptans* 'Burgundy Glow'.

A bright red-pink shrub is accompanied by a contrasting milky-white daffodil and an echoing pink early-flowering tulip. Both the silver lamium and dark-leaved ajuga are semi-evergreen ground-cover plants, which will relish the shade around the shrub, as will the primrose, whose pale yellow flowers look rather good near the deep pink of the shrub.

In early summer, with average to poor and dry, stony soils and a border in full sun, the theme plant is *Papaver orientale* 'Allegro Viva', the secondary plants are *Nepeta* × *faassenii* and *Stachys byzantina*, and the filler plant is *Thymus* × *citriodorus* 'Silver Queen'.

A strongly coloured poppy with large flowers is balanced by the subtle mauve and cloudier effect of the nepeta (catmint). The little thyme with silver-variegated leaves is a cool accompaniment to both.

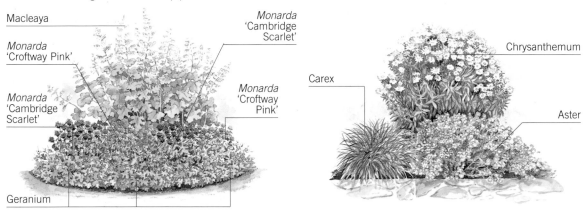

Macleaya · *Monarda* 'Cambridge Scarlet' · *Monarda* 'Croftway Pink' · *Monarda* 'Cambridge Scarlet' · *Monarda* 'Croftway Pink' · Geranium · Chrysanthemum · Carex · Aster

In late summer, with average to damp, reasonably fertile soil and a border in full sun, the theme plants are *Monarda* 'Croftway Pink' and *M.* 'Cambridge Scarlet', the secondary plant is *Macleaya cordata* and the filler plant is *Geranium versicolor* (flowering for a second time after main spring flowering).

The deep colours of monardas look stunning together and the addition of the silvery grey leaves of the macleaya add a cooling contrasting touch.

In early autumn the theme plant is *Leucanthemella serotina* (formerly *Chrysanthemum uliginosum*), the secondary plant is *Aster ericoides* 'Pink Cloud', and the filler plant is *Carex testacea*.

The chrysanthemum's white daisies on tall stems are a true swansong to the floral year. The wispy pink of the aster and the bronze-green of the evergreen sedge add some less spectacular colour and help to add bulk around the rather gawky habit of the chrysanthemum.

people, and to the visually impaired especially, it is essential. It is something that should be asked of every plant that goes into the garden and, ideally, personally investigated. Not only do garden books fail to mention the fragrance of many of the plants they describe, but the descriptions are often so vague and inaccurate that only direct experience can be relied upon.

PLANT GROUPINGS

Any border larger than the very smallest that is composed of one of each variety of plant will not look right: it will seem bitty and unsatisfying. But why is it that some plants look much better than others in groups?

'Plant sociability' is the placing of plants in groups that look satisfying to the majority of onlookers. When you are planning the distribution of plants in a border, it might help to think about which of the following categories you would put each one in.

• **Splendid isolation:** large and medium sized shrubs will obviously overpower, both physically and visually, all but the most enormous borders (and these are unlikely to be yours). Large perennials, such as macleaya, and big grasses, like miscanthus, will do likewise. All you need for plenty of impact is one of each and few of such plants altogether. Those with strong form rather than amorphous bulk — which generally means big perennials and grasses and small shapely trees, rather than shrubs — often look better if they are surrounded by much lower planting. When a plant from this group is at its best it will dominate a planting, so making it a theme plant.

• **Best kept apart:** many small to medium sized shrubs and more particularly perennials about 1–1.5m/3–5ft tall will look good if repeated once or twice in the larger border. Such repetition helps to create a feeling of generous scale. Again, the more distinct the form, the less they should be crowded.

• **Moderately sociable:** many plants look much better when they are grown in small, but loose, groups in medium sized and larger borders. This is more or less true of medium sized perennials and small shrubs about 0.5–1m/1ft 8in–3ft high. Note that most people find odd-numbered groups more pleasing than even-numbered ones. Bear in mind that some plants look fairly untidy after flowering or even, like the popular *Papaver orientale*, go dormant and leave a gap. Such plants should never be grown in tight groups. By group, I do not mean a number of plants that are immediately next to each other but a number of plants that are close enough to have some relation to each other.

• **Definitely need to be together:** there are plants that definitely have to be in groups unless they are to look a bit lonely, except in the smallest borders. Small to medium sized clump formers — approximately 30cm/12in across — have much more impact if they are grown either in clumps or dotted around so that they are close to each other. When these are used as theme plants you will need several of them in the average border if they are to create the desired impact.

• **Never walk alone:** some plants just cannot be grown on their own, even in the smallest borders. Think how absurd a single foxglove looks. Plants that are all vertical and have no horizontals have to be grown in groups for them to look right, however striking they are. The larger the border, the larger the groups should be and, even more importantly if they are theme plants, the more widely distributed such groups should be. Also in this category are small, low-growing, ground-cover plants, often used as filler plants, which lose impact on their own simply because they are small and low.

Old-fashioned roses and honeysuckle provide two of the best loved scents of summer.
Planting them close to a path makes appreciating them easy.

REPETITION AND RHYTHM

Many borders do not succeed because they lack a sense of unity. The worst offenders are those borders where there is an enormous number of different types of plant but no apparent common purpose. It is useful to compare such a border with a roadside of wildflowers. The latter may have only two species in flower but will have more visual impact because the same plants occur throughout, creating a sense of unity. There is no doubt that the most impressive borders are those that repeat a particular plant or plant combination throughout, thus maintaining a sense of common purpose.

When you are planning a border, especially a large one or an elongated one, think about how to develop this sense of unity. Here are some possible ways.

• Part of the idea of including theme plants is to scatter them throughout a border so that the whole is unified. Even more sophisticated is to have a 'theme group', two or three varieties that look simply stunning together and that can be repeated.

• While theme plants may run through a border if they are perennials or bulbs, they cannot be used in this way if one season's predominant plant is a single shrub. Whatever the reason, secondary or filler plants with more subtle colours can be used to unify a border. Think of wildflower meadows: however colourful they are, the most frequent colour is often cream or white or greeny yellow. Such a buffer colour, scattered through a border, will quietly but definitely create a common thread.

Alternatively, a distinctive foliage plant – a purple- or yellow-leaved perennial or a fine-textured ornamental grass, for example – could do the trick instead. Even different plants with similar foliage, all cream variegated for example, can be used in a similar way. The advantage of foliage, especially where there is little space, is that it has a longer season.

• For a year-long repeating element, try using structural plants. Many semi-formal gardens rely for their effect on clipped yew or box shapes, simple pyramids or globes, which are repeated at regular intervals. It does not matter how riotous or wild the rest of the planting is, the discipline of the clipped shrubs will maintain visual order.

GROUPING AND SCATTERING PLANTS

Traditionally perennials and annuals were grown in groups, the belief being that they then had more impact than when they were grown as individuals blending into the overall scheme. Landscapers tend to do the same with shrubs. The results can be successful, but the overall effect is perhaps too formal and heavy-handed for today's more informal look, where the delicacy and subtlety of the cottage garden and wildflower meadow are more highly

Plants with fragrant flowers

	HEIGHT × SPREAD	COLOUR AND SCENT	NOTES
Daphne mezereum	80 × 80cm /32 × 32in	Shrub with scented pink flowers in late winter; white variety also available	Good on alkaline soil; dislikes waterlogging
Heliotropium arborescens hybrids	40 × 40cm /16 × 16in	Distinctive rich scent; purple flowers all summer	A half-hardy perennial; does best in a sheltered site
Matthiola Ten Week Series	30 × 30cm /12 × 12in	Sweetly scented white, red or pink flowers in summer	Usually grown as a hardy annual
Philadelphus 'Innocence'	2 × 2m /6 × 6ft	Shrub with white flowers in early to midsummer; sweetly fragrant, especially in the evening	Tolerant
Rhododendron luteum	2.5 × 2.5m /8 × 8ft	One of many azaleas with rich honey-scented flowers in early summer	This is yellow; pink and orange varieties also available; dislikes lime and drought
Rosa 'Louise Odier'	1.5 × 1m /4 × 3ft	Old-fashioned rose with double, soft pink flowers in early summer; classic rose scent	Some recurrent flowering in autumn

prized. Blending different varieties creates a more naturalistic effect, with co-boundaries blurred rather than groups being clearly separated. Groups of plants can be grown so that they intermingle or actually share space with another group. It is often easier to achieve rhythm and unity in the border by using this approach because there is more scope for scattering individuals through a border.

This intermingling approach works best with perennials and dwarf shrubs, which are either identical to their wild ancestors or similar in habit. Most wild perennials happily intermingle, often depending on each other for physical support, as do many dwarf shrubs that are allowed to grow into each other. Next time you are in a wildflower meadow, a piece of heathland or a stretch of maquis, look at how the wild plants grow.

Highly bred plants such as dwarf varieties of perennials – miniature asters, for example – squat bedding plants – like modern French marigolds – or tightly growing heather varieties are not suitable for this look. Because they are plants with clear

Plants with aromatic foliage

	HEIGHT × SPREAD	COLOUR AND SCENT	NOTES
Helichrysum italicum	0.6 × 1m/2 × 3ft	Curry-scented silver evergreen leaves; yellow flowers in summer	Dislikes poor drainage
Lavandula stoechas 'Pedunculata'	0.7 × 1m/2ft 4in × 3ft	Deliciously scented grey-leaved shrub with dramatic pinkish-mauve flowers in summer	Dislikes damp; needs a sheltered spot
Mentha × piperita 'Citrata'	60 × 60cm/24 × 24in	Eau-de-Cologne scented leaves; purple flowers	Spreading perennial
Myrtus communis	2 × 2m/6 × 6ft (usually less)	Shrub with tiny, dark green evergreen leaves with distinct fragrance; fluffy white flowers	Only suitable for warm, sunny borders
Rosmarinus officinalis	1.5 × 1.5m/5 × 5ft	Shrub with distinctively aromatic dark green, needle-like evergreen leaves; pale blue flowers over a long summer season	Dislikes damp
Santolina chamaecyparissus	0.8 × 1m/2ft 8in × 3ft	Low shrub with fine, silvery-white aromatic leaves; yellow flowers in midsummer	Dislikes damp

Striking, but almost too much: *Clematis* 'Jackmanii', *Salvia × sylvestris* 'Mainacht', a liatris and *Allium sphaerocephalon* are saved from being overpowering by the silver *Eryngium variifolium*.

Plant groupings

One only needed in a border to create impact.

More than one required in larger borders.

Loose groupings create more impact.

There is a definite need for small groups.

Some plants have to be in groups otherwise the impact is completely lost, whether they are tall and narrow plants, like foxgloves, which benefit from having a few scattered individuals outside the main group, or small ground-cover-type plants.

boundaries they need a more formal arrangement of clear groupings. Any other planting scheme will look disorganized.

Planting Plans

Most people start planning by making lists of plants they like. The next step is to check that all these plants will thrive in similar conditions of aspect and site and that they are a suitable size for the border in question. Then there must be some consideration

of whether they are compatible visually – do their colours look good together, for example? We look at questions of height and form on pages 76–86 and of colour on pages 98–114. The next step is to see if you have the seasonal spread of interest that you want, which can be done by drawing up a seasonal spread chart, as on page 60.

If you are now happy with the selection of plants for the border, it may be time to proceed to drawing up a plan. This process will enable you to spend time

Kniphofias and pink *Geranium endressii* combine with annuals to create
an emphatically rhythmic border.

mulling over your selection, thinking about where everything will go and how it will fit into what is already in place. Drawing up a plan is not something that comes easily to everyone, but accuracy is not vital. If accuracy is important or if you want to learn how to do this properly, there are garden design manuals that will show you the basics of drawing up plans.

If paper, pencil and ruler really are alien to you, why not dispense with them altogether and simply mark out planting positions *in situ* on the ground using labels (perhaps coloured to represent the colours of flowers and foliage), measuring the distances between plants using a tape? Most garden designers start by planning the positions of the large structural plants, such as the bigger shrubs and perennials, and then work through the theme plants, before moving on to secondary and filler plants.

A plan will be the first stage in thinking about the numbers of each variety that you will need. Specifically it will show you:

• How plants will relate to each other. Does each plant look good next to its immediate neighbours or, conversely, are there any potential colour clashes or incompatible plants next to each other — for example, is one with a reputation for being invasive next to a slow grower?

• How balanced the whole border will be for seasonal spread, form and colour. Are there spring-flowering plants throughout the border or are they bunched together at one end? Are the strong architectural forms evenly scattered, giving a good backbone to the border? Are the yellows well distributed?

• How the plant distribution relates to the microhabitats found in the border. Is the end shaded by next door's lime tree to be planted with varieties tolerant of dry shade? Is the area with little good soil to have the stress-tolerant lavenders and rock roses?

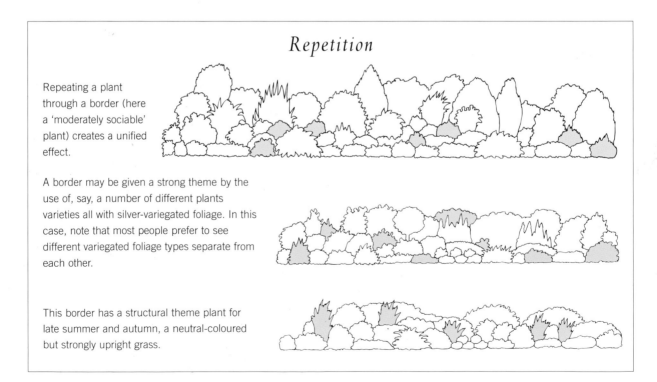

Repetition

Repeating a plant through a border (here a 'moderately sociable' plant) creates a unified effect.

A border may be given a strong theme by the use of, say, a number of different plants varieties all with silver-variegated foliage. In this case, note that most people prefer to see different variegated foliage types separate from each other.

This border has a structural theme plant for late summer and autumn, a neutral-coloured but strongly upright grass.

Two contrasting styles of planting: traditional clumps (above) and the modern style of
intermingled planting (below). The modern style is inspired by the way that wildflowers grow,
although this border is largely filled with bedding annuals.

Grouping in clumps or blending

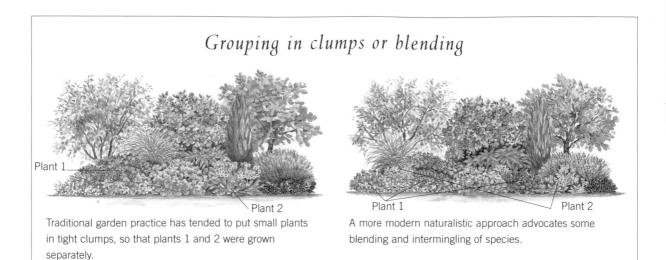

Traditional garden practice has tended to put small plants in tight clumps, so that plants 1 and 2 were grown separately.

A more modern naturalistic approach advocates some blending and intermingling of species.

Planting plans

This planting plan illustrates the use of symbols. Names are used for the larger shrubs, but it is often impracticable to fit names in smaller circles. Numbers can be used, but symbols are the easiest to spot at a glance. The planting is for a blue/white/pink colour scheme to give interest from mid-spring to early autumn, on a soil of average fertility and moisture in full sun. Note how some earlier flowering and more shade-tolerant perennials can be grown so that they partly spread underneath the two larger and more upright growing shrubs.

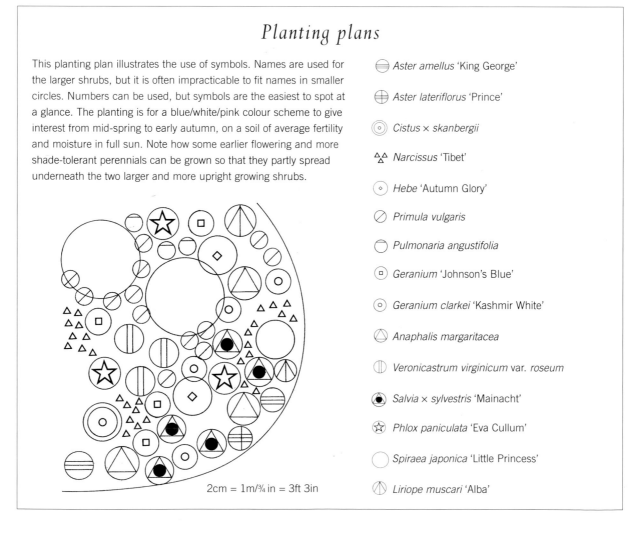

2cm = 1m/¾ in = 3ft 3in

Aster amellus 'King George'

Aster lateriflorus 'Prince'

Cistus × skanbergii

Narcissus 'Tibet'

Hebe 'Autumn Glory'

Primula vulgaris

Pulmonaria angustifolia

Geranium 'Johnson's Blue'

Geranium clarkei 'Kashmir White'

Anaphalis margaritacea

Veronicastrum virginicum var. *roseum*

Salvia × sylvestris 'Mainacht'

Phlox paniculata 'Eva Cullum'

Spiraea japonica 'Little Princess'

Liriope muscari 'Alba'

5

Seasonal Interest

Making a border that is colourful and interesting in spring or summer is easy, but planning a border that has these attributes in late autumn and winter is more of a challenge, and what really takes skill is creating a border that is interesting all year round. Having a border that looks like something straight out of a flower show every day of the year is perhaps an unreasonable demand, but at least we can make something that is always a credit to our ability to choose plants. The smaller the border the more difficult it is to pack in something for every month of the year, and yet if you have a tiny garden this may be your only growing space. It is vital not only that it looks reasonably attractive all year round but also that it has nothing in it that is going to let it down. A perennial that looks scruffy after flowering may not be noticed in a big border but certainly will be in a small one.

The traditional way of keeping a border looking cheerful all the year round is a programme of

Papaver orientale (oriental poppy) is spectacular in bloom but becomes dormant by midsummer. Something else will be needed to fill the gaps it leaves.

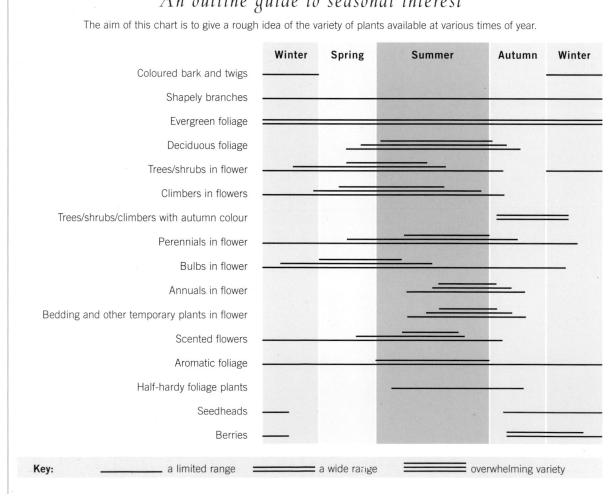

An outline guide to seasonal interest

The aim of this chart is to give a rough idea of the variety of plants available at various times of year.

	Winter	Spring	Summer	Autumn	Winter
Coloured bark and twigs					
Shapely branches					
Evergreen foliage					
Deciduous foliage					
Trees/shrubs in flower					
Climbers in flowers					
Trees/shrubs/climbers with autumn colour					
Perennials in flower					
Bulbs in flower					
Annuals in flower					
Bedding and other temporary plants in flower					
Scented flowers					
Aromatic foliage					
Half-hardy foliage plants					
Seedheads					
Berries					

Key: ———— a limited range   ═══════ a wide range   ═══════ overwhelming variety

Seasonal interest

By charting the season of interest of plants on a list it may be seen at a glance where there are gaps. If the lines are coloured to represent flower and – if you feel it relevant – foliage colour, the colour combinations at any given time can be seen. Do not forget to add factors other than flower and leaf colour: there is autumn foliage and berry colour, too, the colour of young shoots in spring and coloured bark and twigs in the winter. Plant form can be added as well if you wish.

	Winter	Spring	Summer	Autumn	Winter
Trees/shrubs					
Amelanchier lamarckii					
Hamamelis mollis					
Juniperus communis 'Hibernica'					
Rosa rugosa 'Fru Dagmar Hastrup'					
Dwarf shrubs					
Erica carnea 'December Red'					
Erica carnea 'Springood White'					
Erica carnea 'Vivellii'					
Climbers					
Clematis viticella 'Madame Julia Correvon'					
Hedera helix 'Glacier' (cream & gold variegated foliage)					
Lonicera × americana					
Perennials					
Ajuga reptans					
Alchemilla mollis					
Aster cordifolius					
Aster ericoides					
Aster lateriflorus 'Horizontalis'					
Astrantia major					
Campanula persicifolia					
Convallaria majalis					
Geranium endressii					
Geranium 'Johnson's Blue'					
Geranium phaeum					
Helleborus hybrids (flowers in various colours)					
Lamium maculatum (white & silver variegated foliage)					
Monarda 'Capricorn'					
Monarda 'Pisces'					
Persicaria amplexicaulis					
Primula (polyanthus types; flowers in various colours)					
Pulmonaria angustifolia					
Verbena bonariensis					
Bulbs					
Crocus 'Cream Beauty'					
Crocus 'E.A. Bowles'					
Crocus vernus					
Erythronium californicum 'White Beauty'					
Fritillaria meleagris					
Galanthus nivalis					
Hyacinthoides non-scripta					
Lilium martagon					
Lilium martagon var. *album*					
Muscari neglectum					
Narcissus 'Actea'					
Narcissus 'Mount Hood'					
Narcissus 'Rembrandt'					
Grasses					
Carex comans bronze form					
Carex dipsacea					
Luzula nivea					
Melica altissima 'Atropurpurea'					
Miscanthus sinensis 'Gracillimus'					
Molinia caerulea ssp. *caerulea* 'Heidebraut'					
Annuals					
Brachycome iberidifolia					
Matthiola Ten Week Series					
Nigella damascena 'Persian Jewels'					
Rhodochiton atrosanguineus (half-hardy annual climber, grown as a scrambler)					
Verbena 'Pink Parfait'					

labour-intensive planting out and replacement, so that summer bedding plants are put in in late spring, removed in autumn and replaced by winter bedding plants and bulbs, which would flower in spring. Quite apart from the amount of work involved, this approach has some serious drawbacks. During winter the bedding plants, almost invariably pansies or polyanthus, are never quite up to it, and there is a gap during late spring and early summer, which is a great irony when you consider that wildflowers are at their best at this time. There is no doubt that herbaceous perennials, shrubs and bulbs chosen for their ability to perform in the prevailing climate and conditions are able to give much better year-round performance.

Despite the obvious inadequacies of the traditional approach there are, however, lessons to be learned from it, especially by those with the time and inclination to do some seasonal replanting. The trick is to combine the bedding-out approach with having a good, solid and permanent framework, so that the temporary planting is seen as, if you will, the icing on the cake. There is no doubt that such an approach can result in a more intensely coloured border over a longer season. Whatever approach you adopt, however, the crucial thing is to ensure that seasonal interest is interwoven so that, as one plant finishes, another close to it takes over.

As far as the permanent framework is concerned, a large part of good planting is simply being aware of what is available. It is surprising how many gardeners complain that there is little in flower in late summer and autumn, largely because late-flowering perennials are somewhat out of fashion and thus not often seen. Visiting gardens that are open to the public is one invaluable and rewarding way that you can become aware of previously unfamiliar or currently unfashionable plants.

Many gardeners keep a notebook of plants that they have seen or have heard about and that they intend to try to get hold of the next time they are doing some new planting. If you look at your list and make a selection of plants that satisfies you in terms of factors such as the combination of colour and foliage, your next task should be to look critically at its seasonal spread by making a chart such as the one on page 60.

Once you have made a selection of plants, you must plan where they are to go. This is crucial if you are to have a good seasonal spread, particularly in small borders, because of the way that plants can be layered so that as the year progresses different varieties can be used to hide each other or intermingle so that even the smallest space is never dull.

Traditionally, plants in gardens have been grown so that they rather separate from each other, yet if the gardener looks at how plants grow in nature, all kinds of lessons can be learned, particularly how plants grow together, which has considerable importance for how plants are placed in borders to ensure a long season of flowering.

BULBS AND PERENNIALS

Many winter- and spring-flowering plants are bulbs or low perennials, which take advantage of the lack of leaves on deciduous trees to flower and grow. These are the kind of plants that can be put under trees and shrubs to fill spaces that will otherwise look bare at this time. During the rest of the year, when the woody plants are in leaf, the bulbs will have retreated underground and the perennial plants like pulmonarias and primulas will welcome the shade. They may be more or less hidden, but in many cases this does not matter because they will not be looking at their best anyway.

Summer-flowering perennials can be surrounded

Best seasonal plants

Winter	HEIGHT × SPREAD	COLOUR AND SCENT	NOTES
Carex testacea	50 × 50cm/20 × 20in	Grass-like, olive-green leaves in a neat tuft become more orange as winter progresses	Best if blended with perennials; *C. dipsacea* is similar
Cyclamen coum	6 × 10cm/2½ × 4in	Tuber with red, pink or white flowers and neat oval leaves	Needs light shade; good for underplanting shrubs
Erica carnea varieties	30 × 60cm/1 × 2ft	Low, shrubby heather varieties with red, pink or white flowers	Need sun and good drainage; will grow on lime; good for front of borders
Galanthus nivalis (snowdrop)	8 × 6cm/3¼ × 6½in	White flowers; clump forming	Essential for under-planting trees, shrubs and late-emerging perennials
Rubus cockburnianus	2.5 × 2.5m/8 × 8ft	White bloom on upright stems catches low winter light	Not particularly attractive in summer; best at back of the border
Viburnum tinus	3 × 3m/10 × 10ft	Neat, evergreen shrub; white flowers appear early	Good for back of the border
Spring (see also spring bulbs, page 129)			
Camellia 'Donation'	2 × 2m/6 × 6ft (can get larger in mild areas)	Pink flowers on glossy evergreen shrub	Best on lime-free, moist but well-drained soil; prefers light shade
Euphorbia characias ssp. *wulfenii*	1.2 × 1.2m/4 × 4ft	Shrubby perennial with grey evergreen leaves; yellow-green flowers over a long period	Invaluable in a number of border situations; likes sun and good drainage; tolerates dry shade
Magnolia stellata	2.5 × 2.5m/8 × 8ft	Shrub with masses of starry white flowers	Best in light shade on moist, well-drained soil
Primula vulgaris	20 × 30cm/4 × 12in	Pale yellow flowers above rosettes of evergreen leaves	Good for underplanting shrubs and scattering among larger, late-emerging perennials
Ribes sanguineum	2 × 1.5m/6 × 5ft	Deep pink flowers on an upright shrub	Good in light shade; best at back of border
Viburnum × *juddii*	1.2 × 1.5m/4 × 5ft	Deliciously scented white flowers in late spring	Tolerates light shade

Best seasonal plants (continued)

Early and midsummer	HEIGHT × SPREAD	COLOUR AND SCENT	NOTES
Cistus × cyprius	1.5 × 1.5m/5 × 5ft	Large white flowers with central markings	Magnificent shrub for warm, sunny border
Elymus magellanicus	40 × 50cm/16 × 20in	The bluest leaved plant there is; neat, non-spreading tufts of more or less evergreen grassy leaves	Ideal for dotting around the border between perennials
Exochorda × macrantha 'The Bride'	1.5 × 3m/5 × 10ft	Spreading shrub with masses of white flowers	Good for tumbling over the front of the border
Geranium 'Johnson's Blue'	50 × 60cm/20 × 24in	Perennial with mauve-blue flowers over neat foliage	Suitable for front and middle of border
Kolkwitzia amabilis	3 × 3m/10 × 10ft	Masses of pink flowers; yellow autumn leaves	Shrub that can be grown at back of the border or trained on a wall or fence to reduce space required
Matteucia struthiopteris	70 × 60cm/28 × 24in	Fern with wonderfully delicate, fresh green fronds	Looks best among low-growing plants in moist shade
Late summer			
Ceratostigma willmottianum	1 × 1m/3 × 3ft	Pure blue flowers on a neat shrub; good autumn colour	Dislikes extreme cold
Knautia macedonica	70 × 60cm/28 × 24in	Perennial with unique deep pinkish-red flowers that combine well with other colours	Likes sun; suitable for poor soils
Lavatera 'Rosea'	2 × 2.5m/6 × 8ft	Fast-growing but short-lived shrub with masses of pink flowers all summer	Spectacular but can overwhelm small borders; liable to damage in cold winters
Perovskia atriplicifolia	1 × 0.5m/3ft × 1ft 8in	Richly aromatic foliage and lovely blue-mauve flowers in late summer	Needs sun and good drainage
Phygelius capensis var. coccineus	1.5 × 1.5m/5 × 5ft	Tubular, scarlet flowers	Shrub but best treated as herbaceous in cold areas; needs sun
Rubus 'Benenden'	3 × 2m/10 × 6ft	Large white flowers on an upright shrub	Good for back of border; tolerates light shade

Best seasonal plants (continued)

Autumn	HEIGHT × SPREAD	FLOWERS AND FOLIAGE	NOTES
Acer palmatum	5 × 5m/16 × 16ft	Best source of autumn colour in the border	Numerous varieties available, including dwarf forms
Colchicum autumnale	15 × 20cm/6 × 8in	Bulb with pink, crocus-like flowers	Leaves do not appear until spring and take a lot of room; best for mid-border
Euonymus alatus	2 × 2m/6 × 6ft	Vivid scarlet leaves and pendent pink fruit	Good overall shape
Pennisetum villosum	40 × 70cm/16 × 28in	Soft, feathery grass in mounds	Superb for front of border; dislikes damp winters and cold, wet areas
Pyracantha 'Orange Glow'	4 × 3m/13 × 10ft (but can be kept smaller by clipping)	Dense shrubs with evergreen foliage and fiery berries	Needs sun
Sorbus vilmorinii	4 × 3m/13 × 10ft	Startling pink berries; bronze autumn colour	Small tree, ideal centrepiece for island bed

by bulbs in a similar way. The traditional herbaceous border may be dull in spring, with only dead sticks and a few tiny shoots visible above bare soil. But flowering bulbs, scattered through the border from back to front, will transform it. Snowdrops can start the year, followed by crocuses, daffodils and narcissi and then by tulips, which will coincide with the first herbaceous perennials of summer. When their flowers have finished and their foliage is beginning to look a mess, the perennials will start to grow and take over. Low-growing, more or less evergreen perennials like primulas can be used in a similar way, but only if they are not going to be smothered by the often expansive growth of summer-flowering perennials.

SHRUBS AND PERENNIALS

Winter- and spring-flowering shrubs may be welcome, but many gardeners feel that they take up an inordinate amount of border space afterwards, looking dull, if not downright untidy, throughout summer. Pruning – after flowering is the best time for the majority of such shrubs – will restrict their size to some extent, but you might want to consider using other plants to conceal them to some extent. We are familiar from country walks with the way in which many perennial wildflowers and deciduous climbers, practically invisible during winter, suddenly become visible, often showily so, in summer. Perennials have a great role to play here, not just in providing flowers for the summer border but to grow in front of shrubs that are past their best.

Clever layering of perennials in the border can be used to conceal those species that deteriorate in appearance after flowering. Earlier flowering perennials, such as hardy geraniums, most of which look their best in early summer, can often look scruffy later on, especially if they flop or fall apart in the middle. Later flowering and sometimes taller perennials, such as asters and monardas, can be used to screen them if they are planted in front, with the majority of earlier flowering ones in the middle and back of the border. Such later flowering varieties are almost always tidy until after they flower and are often quite insignificant until they do so, being merely clumps of green foliage. This goes against the old adage of 'tallest at the back, shortest at the front', but that precept had currency in an age when

there was time to trim back plants that had finished flowering. A border with a solid screen of tall plants at the front at the end of the season would look odd, though. What is needed is to have a few of these plants dotted around the front half of the border so that they become the centre of attention rather than the faded specimens immediately behind them or to use medium sized – say 30–50cm/12–20in high – varieties of late-flowering perennials like dwarf Michaelmas daisies (varieties of *Aster novi-belgii*) in the front row.

Spring can be an extremely colourful time of year, and it is, for a number
of reasons, easier at this time of year than in later seasons to combine strong colours, such
as polyanthus, muscari and tulips.

CLIMBERS

It used to be the case that the only place in the garden where climbers were found was trained against walls or fences. Alternatively, they were occasionally allowed to drape themselves decoratively over old fruit trees that were way past their best. In nature climbers are usually seen in this latter role, clambering over trees and shrubs so that they can reach up to the light. Increasing numbers of gardeners are experimenting with them in this way, having discovered that this is a good way of getting two lots of flowering out of the same space.

A shrub or tree that flowers in spring can have a climber growing up through and over it to flower in summer and even, if it is large and strong enough, more than one, with different flowering seasons. Not every climber is suitable; wisterias and climbing roses that get too big are obviously going to do more harm than good and are suitable for growing up only the largest trees. The climber must be chosen so that it is small and light enough to be supported by the host, which must also be a well-established specimen. The best ones to choose are those that, like many clematis, are deciduous and are

LEFT: Mid- to late summer is a particularly good time for 'hot' colours, such as the hemerocallis and ligularia against a background of the shrub cotinus.
ABOVE: Moody purples and pinks in an early autumn mist. Asters and dahlias glow with the hips of *Rosa glauca* in the background

A rime of ice crystals brings an extra dimension to the sculptural forms of the last season's perennials.
Cutting back such plants in autumn would mean losing an important aspect of winter beauty.

Permanent planting

A cross-section of a border planted for a good seasonal spread without using annuals or temporary planting.

Winter
1. *Buxus sempervirens* 'Suffruticosa' – evergreen
2. *Aster thomsonii* 'Nanus' – dormant
3. *Galanthus nivalis* – beginning to flower
4. *Echinops bannaticus* 'Taplow Blue' – dormant
5. *Narcissus* 'Mount Hood' – shoots emerging
6. *Geranium endressii* – some green shoots
7. *Pulmonaria rubra* – evergreen, beginning to flower
8. *Chaenomeles speciosa* 'Nivalis' – beginning to flower, leafless
9. *Clematis* 'Bill MacKenzie' – dormant, leafless

Spring
1. *Buxus sempervirens* 'Suffruticosa' – evergreen
2. *Aster thomsonii* 'Nanus' – shoots emerging
3. *Galanthus nivalis* – finishing flowering
4. *Echinops bannaticus* 'Taplow Blue' – shoots emerging
5. *Narcissus* 'Mount Hood' – flowering
6. *Geranium endressii* – green leaves
7. *Pulmonaria rubra* – flowering
8. *Chaenomeles speciosa* 'Nivalis' – flowering, leaves emerging
9. *Clematis* 'Bill MacKenzie' – leaves emerging

Early summer
1. *Buxus sempervirens* 'Suffruticosa' – evergreen
2. *Aster thomsonii* 'Nanus' – clump of leaves
3. *Galanthus nivalis* – dormant
4. *Echinops bannaticus* 'Taplow Blue' – clump of leaves
5. *Narcissus* 'Mount Hood' – leaves dying back
6. *Geranium endressii* – flowering
7. *Pulmonaria rubra* – leaves
8. *Chaenomeles speciosa* 'Nivalis' – in leaf
9. *Clematis* 'Bill MacKenzie' in leaf, some shoots beginning to venture over 8

Early autumn
1. *Buxus sempervirens* 'Suffruticosa' – evergreen
2. *Aster thomsonii* 'Nanus' – flowering
3. *Galanthus nivalis* dormant
4. *Echinops bannaticus* 'Taplow Blue' – finished flowering, but seedheads a strong feature
5. *Narcissus* 'Mount Hood' – dormant
6. *Geranium endressii* – second flowering on rather sprawling clump
7. *Pulmonaria rubra* – leaves
8. *Chaenomeles speciosa* 'Nivalis' – in leaf, partially covered with stems of 9
9. *Clematis* 'Bill MacKenzie' – flowering*

*Note: This particular clematis is a vigorous climber and should not be allowed to scramble over shrubs unless they are well established; in any event, such growths should be pruned clear of the shrub annually.

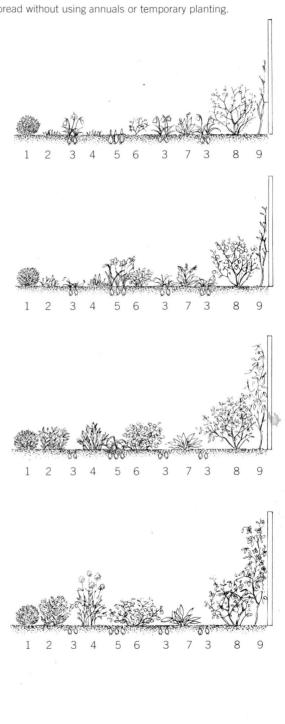

Permanent and temporary planting

A cross-section of a border planted for a good seasonal spread using annuals
and other temporary planting in a framework of permanent plants.

Late winter/early spring

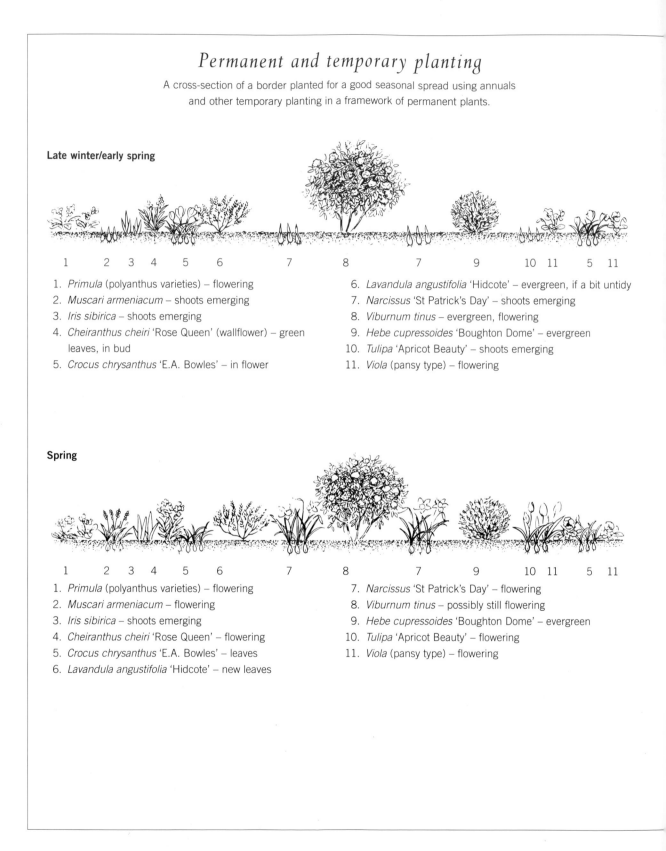

1 2 3 4 5 6 7 8 7 9 10 11 5 11

1. *Primula* (polyanthus varieties) – flowering
2. *Muscari armeniacum* – shoots emerging
3. *Iris sibirica* – shoots emerging
4. *Cheiranthus cheiri* 'Rose Queen' (wallflower) – green leaves, in bud
5. *Crocus chrysanthus* 'E.A. Bowles' – in flower
6. *Lavandula angustifolia* 'Hidcote' – evergreen, if a bit untidy
7. *Narcissus* 'St Patrick's Day' – shoots emerging
8. *Viburnum tinus* – evergreen, flowering
9. *Hebe cupressoides* 'Boughton Dome' – evergreen
10. *Tulipa* 'Apricot Beauty' – shoots emerging
11. *Viola* (pansy type) – flowering

Spring

1 2 3 4 5 6 7 8 7 9 10 11 5 11

1. *Primula* (polyanthus varieties) – flowering
2. *Muscari armeniacum* – flowering
3. *Iris sibirica* – shoots emerging
4. *Cheiranthus cheiri* 'Rose Queen' – flowering
5. *Crocus chrysanthus* 'E.A. Bowles' – leaves
6. *Lavandula angustifolia* 'Hidcote' – new leaves
7. *Narcissus* 'St Patrick's Day' – flowering
8. *Viburnum tinus* – possibly still flowering
9. *Hebe cupressoides* 'Boughton Dome' – evergreen
10. *Tulipa* 'Apricot Beauty' – flowering
11. *Viola* (pansy type) – flowering

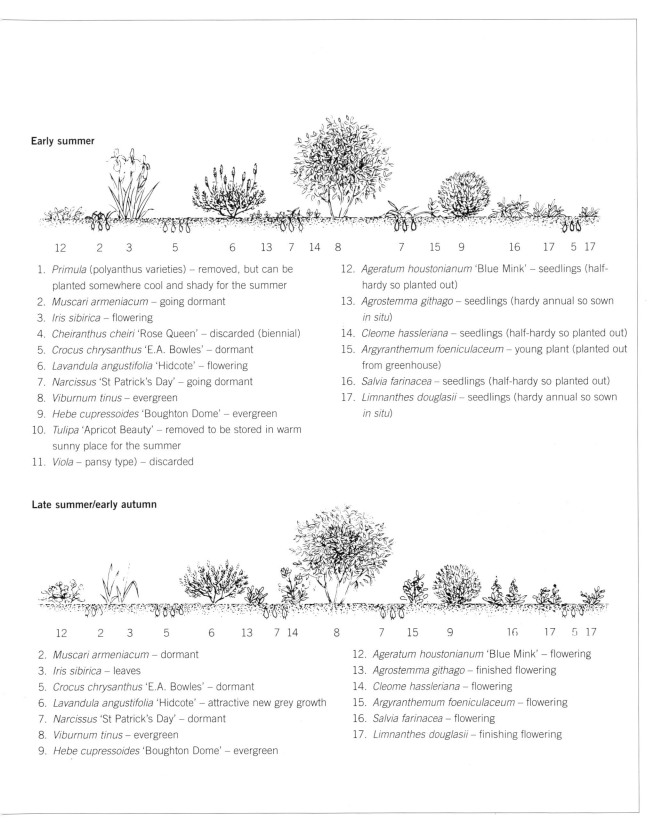

Early summer

12   2   3   5   6   13   7   14   8   7   15   9   16   17   5   17

1. *Primula* (polyanthus varieties) – removed, but can be planted somewhere cool and shady for the summer
2. *Muscari armeniacum* – going dormant
3. *Iris sibirica* – flowering
4. *Cheiranthus cheiri* 'Rose Queen' – discarded (biennial)
5. *Crocus chrysanthus* 'E.A. Bowles' – dormant
6. *Lavandula angustifolia* 'Hidcote' – flowering
7. *Narcissus* 'St Patrick's Day' – going dormant
8. *Viburnum tinus* – evergreen
9. *Hebe cupressoides* 'Boughton Dome' – evergreen
10. *Tulipa* 'Apricot Beauty' – removed to be stored in warm sunny place for the summer
11. *Viola* – pansy type) – discarded

12. *Ageratum houstonianum* 'Blue Mink' – seedlings (half-hardy so planted out)
13. *Agrostemma githago* – seedlings (hardy annual so sown *in situ*)
14. *Cleome hassleriana* – seedlings (half-hardy so planted out)
15. *Argyranthemum foeniculaceum* – young plant (planted out from greenhouse)
16. *Salvia farinacea* – seedlings (half-hardy so planted out)
17. *Limnanthes douglasii* – seedlings (hardy annual so sown *in situ*)

Late summer/early autumn

12   2   3   5   6   13   7   14   8   7   15   9   16   17   5   17

2. *Muscari armeniacum* – dormant
3. *Iris sibirica* – leaves
5. *Crocus chrysanthus* 'E.A. Bowles' – dormant
6. *Lavandula angustifolia* 'Hidcote' – attractive new grey growth
7. *Narcissus* 'St Patrick's Day' – dormant
8. *Viburnum tinus* – evergreen
9. *Hebe cupressoides* 'Boughton Dome' – evergreen

12. *Ageratum houstonianum* 'Blue Mink' – flowering
13. *Agrostemma githago* – finished flowering
14. *Cleome hassleriana* – flowering
15. *Argyranthemum foeniculaceum* – flowering
16. *Salvia farinacea* – flowering
17. *Limnanthes douglasii* – finishing flowering

generally kept pruned back during winter. They will thus be practically invisible until late spring when growth begins.

It is even possible to use small-growing climbers with light growth – *Clematis viticella* varieties, for example – as trailers and scramblers over low-growing shrubs. A particularly successful combination is to have them growing loosely over winter-flowering heathers (*Erica carnea* varieties) so that you get two seasons' worth of flower out of one place.

ANNUALS AND BEDDING PLANTS FOR LATE-SEASON COLOUR

Annuals or plants grown as annuals, such as many bedding plants, have been a much-loved source of late-summer, often vibrant colour, and as increasing numbers of new introductions become available these plants are set to become even more popular. In the past there were two clear categories – hardy annuals and half-hardy annuals – but now the situation is more complex. Hardy annuals mostly have cottage garden associations and are sown where they are to flower, while half-hardies are started off under glass and then 'bedded out' for summer, often being bought as young plants from garden centres. Recent years have seen the arrival of a much wider range of slightly tender plants, the so-called patio plants, which are sold for temporary summer planting but which can often be kept over winter.

The advantage of all these plants is that they look their best towards the end of the season, from midsummer until the first frosts, and, being rapid growers, they make ideal temporary space fillers. If they are used traditionally *en masse* there is a dull period of several weeks until they are established and flowering, but when they are used as mixed border plants they can be inserted into plantings to take over once the permanent border plants have finished.

Such an approach is, of course, more labour intensive than relying completely on permanent elements, but it results in an undeniably more colourful and vibrant border, which may, in a small garden, be what is wanted. Keen gardeners may prefer to grow their own half-hardy annuals from seed, but many will choose to buy them ready grown from garden centres. The more expensive patio plants can usually be kept from year to year if they are dug up in autumn and overwintered in a greenhouse or cold frame. Alternatively, they can be propagated from cuttings taken in midsummer, which may be more easy to keep going over winter; several pots of rooted cuttings can be fitted on to the smallest windowsill. Taking your own cuttings, which is nearly always extremely easy with these plants, enables you to use these varieties extensively in the border at a fraction of the cost of buying them in each year.

However they are obtained, the young plants need careful planting. The perennials that have finished flowering must be cut back and tidied up in order to make space for the new arrivals. This tidying up must be followed by good soil preparation and the provision of adequate nutrients in the form of compost or fertilizers.

Hardy annuals, which are usually sown where they are to flower, can also be treated in a similar way to half-hardy plants, and raised in pots or seed trays before being planted out as young plants. Such an approach avoids the empty period of several months that results from growing them from seed *in situ*. It has to be said, however, that they do establish themselves better when the seed is sown directly in the ground in the traditional manner, and bedding them out from pot-grown plants will be completely successful only where there is no danger of summer drought.

6

Structuring and Composing the Border

A BORDER FILLED WITH colourful flowers may look wonderful at first sight, but if it is all colour and no structure it will begin to look a bit formless or even untidy on a closer examination, and when the flowers fade it can really look a mess.

A border is just like a painting, which has to be composed and which will look so much better if this is done skilfully. Are the plants in your border going to vary much in height? Are the tallest plants going to be at the back? What shapes are going to be dominant? How are the shapes going to relate to each other? These questions have nothing to do with flowers and colour; they are about something more fundamental. A colourful but structureless border is a greater failure than one that is well structured but that has a poor colour scheme. People's opinions on colour are so idiosyncratic that someone is sure to like even the most garish collection of plants, but an ill-structured border will be revealed the minute the flowers fade.

Getting the structure right is easier than devising a colour scheme, yet getting the information to do it well is not always easy. Gardening reference books are often uninformative about a plant's shape, and this is something that is invariably impossible to tell from looking at a few twigs in a pot in the garden centre.

Nothing can teach you so much about structure as looking at plants in other people's gardens, with well-established gardens being particularly good places for appreciating the shapes and eventual sizes of mature shrubs and trees.

Not only do the colours contrast effectively but so do the forms of these oriental poppies, peonies, lupins and hardy geraniums.

HEIGHT

Height is all about visibility and proportion. A tall plant in the wrong place not only looks out of place but stops you seeing anything behind it. On the other hand, this characteristic can be useful at times. If you have a particularly long border, for example, you may want to divide it up so that not all of it is seen at once, perhaps keeping a surprise around the corner.

The height of the plants in a border needs to relate to the size of both the border and the garden. A small garden or border is easily overwhelmed by several tall plants – there is a sense of a toddler trying to walk in its parent's shoes. It is important to distinguish between height and bulk, however: a tall, slender plant, such as the Rocky Mountain juniper (*Juniperus scopulorum* 'Skyrocket'), can magically add height but its lack of bulk means that it does not impose itself. On the other hand, a small border may be built around one particularly good small tree or large shrub, and if it looks good all year round why not be proud of it and make it the theme plant, letting it dictate the rest of the scheme? The foliage and flower colours of the other denizens of the border will need to complement this plant. A good example might be a shrub with golden foliage surrounded by other yellow-leaved plants and plenty of complementary blue or mauve flowers.

What about the opposite situation: a large border full of low plants? The setting here is important, for a 'big' or grand landscape demands big borders but not necessarily borders that are filled with large plants. Large border plants work well with large buildings, helping to add a sense of balance, but

Plants for vertical emphasis

	HEIGHT × SPREAD	COLOUR AND SCENT	NOTES
Calamagrostis × acutiflora 'Karl Foerster'	1.2 × 0.4m/4ft × 1ft 4in	Strongly upright, pale brown heads	Superb vertical emphasis among lower planting for late summer to winter
Digitalis purpurea (foxglove)	1.5 × 0.3m/5 × 1ft	Spikes of pink-purple or white flowers	Short lived but will self-seed; grows in light shade or sun
Eremurus robustus	2 × 0.6m/6 × 2ft	Imposing spikes with masses of tiny pink flowers	Leaves die back in summer; does best in hot, dry situations
Juniperus scopulorum 'Skyrocket'	6 × 0.7m/20ft × 2ft 4in	Dark grey-green	Narrow conifer like a smaller, hardier version of the classic Italian cypress
Semiarundinaria fastuosa (Narihira bamboo)	5 × 2m/16 × 6ft	Elegant green foliage	One of many bamboos for creating verticals; good for the back of moist, lightly shaded borders
Taxus baccata 'Fastigiata' (Irish yew)	10 × 4m/33 × 13ft	Dark, glossy needles; red berries in autumn	Can be kept clipped and tied with wire to form narrow specimen

Height in the border

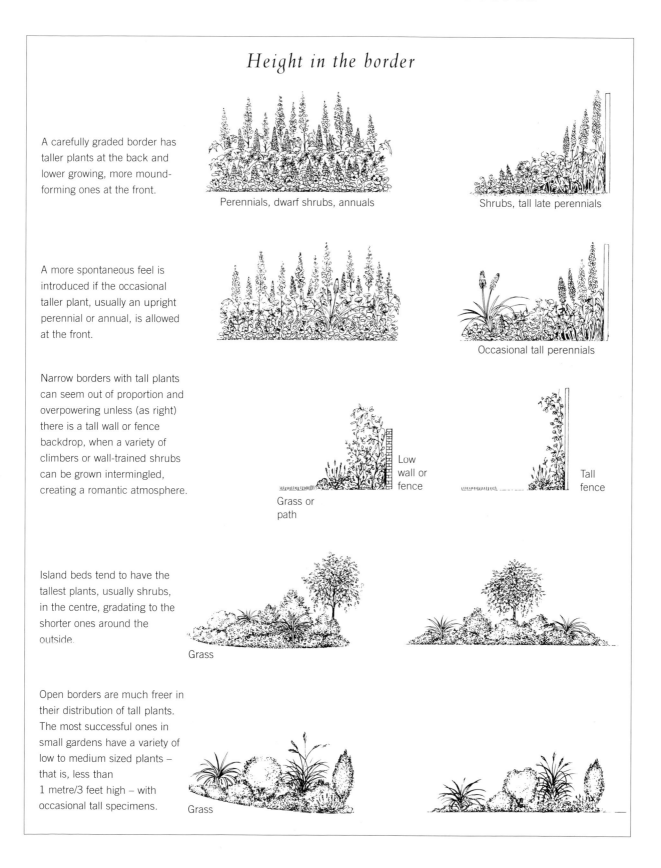

A carefully graded border has taller plants at the back and lower growing, more mound-forming ones at the front.

Perennials, dwarf shrubs, annuals

Shrubs, tall late perennials

A more spontaneous feel is introduced if the occasional taller plant, usually an upright perennial or annual, is allowed at the front.

Occasional tall perennials

Narrow borders with tall plants can seem out of proportion and overpowering unless (as right) there is a tall wall or fence backdrop, when a variety of climbers or wall-trained shrubs can be grown intermingled, creating a romantic atmosphere.

Low wall or fence

Grass or path

Tall fence

Island beds tend to have the tallest plants, usually shrubs, in the centre, gradating to the shorter ones around the outside.

Grass

Open borders are much freer in their distribution of tall plants. The most successful ones in small gardens have a variety of low to medium sized plants – that is, less than 1 metre/3 feet high – with occasional tall specimens.

Grass

Creating height in the border

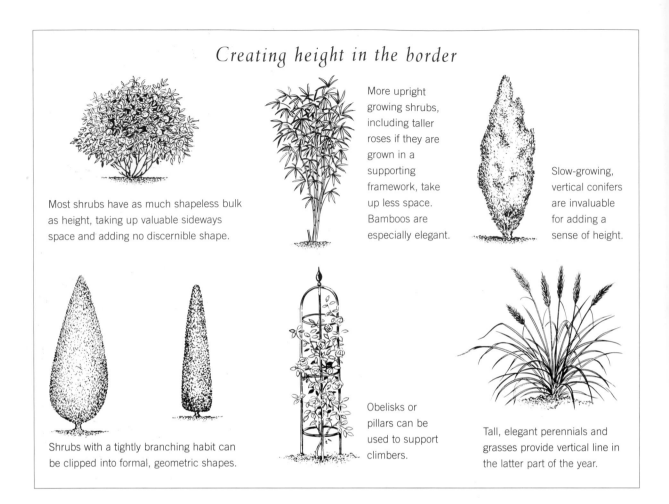

Most shrubs have as much shapeless bulk as height, taking up valuable sideways space and adding no discernible shape.

More upright growing shrubs, including taller roses if they are grown in a supporting framework, take up less space. Bamboos are especially elegant.

Slow-growing, vertical conifers are invaluable for adding a sense of height.

Shrubs with a tightly branching habit can be clipped into formal, geometric shapes.

Obelisks or pillars can be used to support climbers.

Tall, elegant perennials and grasses provide vertical line in the latter part of the year.

wide, open landscapes are different. If it is a lush, fertile landscape, large plants seem appropriate, but if it is open or, especially, if it is windswept, not only will the plants suffer (and tall perennials most of all) but they may look inappropriate as well. Low borders containing short perennials and dwarf shrubs may be more in keeping.

As we noted in the previous chapter, the old rule in border planting was to have a neat gradation in height from the back to the front or, in the case of the island bed, from the centre to the outside. This type of arrangement was not only tidy and ordered but, in theory, allowed everything to be seen. A planting scheme like this works well in formal settings, and it can be immensely satisfying to achieve

– it is not that easy! – but it is not necessarily the best way to display plants. If it is a 'one-season' border, made up of mid- to late-summer-flowering perennials combined with annuals and bedding plants, it can work well. But for a border that aims to provide interest for as long a season as possible, it does not work well. For a start, early-flowering perennials tend to be lower growing while later flowering ones are taller, and then, of course, a lot of plants look untidy after flowering and we don't particularly want to keep on looking at them.

Even in the most carefully angled border, it can be a good idea to have some taller plants near the front, just to offer a little diversion. Tall, thin ones, pillars and columns rather than bulky shapes, are best. Several of the perennials that regularly self-seed – aquilegias, fennel or caper spurge (*Euphorbia lathyris*), for example – are especially good in this respect. In sowing themselves they add a little natural design to the border.

With modern informal, open borders, in which perennials predominate, height is something seasonal. Spring starts the season with low splashes of colour, and as the year warms and progresses so the perennials and ornamental grasses grow taller, ending with some topping 2 metres/6 feet or so. This seasonal growth is something that can radically change the appearance of a garden over the year. Perennials within such a planting need to be scattered so that not too many tall plants are together and so that, as the viewer walks around, new vistas across the planting are opened up. Whatever the format of the border, however, perennials have one great advantage over shrubs: the speed with which they reach their maximum height, usually in the second year after planting.

In most borders, though, it is shrubs rather than perennials that are relied on to provide height. In the opinion of most gardeners, their advantage over perennials is that they are permanent. Their presence seems to many to be essential to the structure of a border, and even when the shrubs are deciduous, their skeletal winter presence adds height and bulk to the border. It may be considered unfortunate that most shrubs grow in such a formless way, and getting shrubs to contribute strong shape as well as height to a border is an important aspect of good border management.

SHAPE

A well-planted border should give pleasure from wherever it is viewed. Just as the colour and formation of individual flowers, and especially their scent,

Flower colour, foliage colour and shape and plant form combine to create an exceptionally strong planting.

can be appreciated close up, so the overall shape of the plants in the border should delight from a distance. Shape is something that is best understood and appreciated at times when the effect of colour is reduced: in the dim light of daybreak or dusk or at those times of year when there is little in flower. Shape is vitally important in winter, for without it a border will be no more attractive than a damp field. This is one reason why the mixed border is the centrepiece of the modern garden: the old-fashioned, purely herbaceous perennial borders had nothing to offer for winter.

The key words in the successful combining of shapes in the border are 'contrast' and 'harmony'. A one-colour border – all pink flowers, for instance – is rarely dull and is, in fact, almost certain to be successful, but a border composed entirely of one particular plant shape is likely to be rather monotonous or even, if strong, spiky shapes predominate, rather tiring to the eye.

A cursory look at most plants, woody or herbaceous, will quite quickly bring home the fact that they do not have particularly strong shapes. They grow in an amorphous way, rarely unattractive but never outstanding. Plants with good shapes may be relatively few and far between, but they are of immeasurable value when it comes to planning an interesting border. Only a few are needed, perhaps only one in a small border, but the effect they can have is often out of all proportion to their number. Evergreens such as conifers and laurels are as useful for their shape as their leaves – consider, for instance, the column of a narrow juniper or cypress or the neat globe of a dwarf thuja or clipped box.

It is useful to divide plant shapes into the formal and informal. The former are predictably neat and tidy, and if they can grow evenly and more or less symmetrically they will. The popular dwarf conifers are invaluable in this respect. Plants with an informal shape may be amorphous or they may be interesting and sculptural, but they are not naturally even in growth. An example might be the evergreen

Plants with sculptural form

	HEIGHT × SPREAD	FLOWERS AND FOLIAGE	NOTES
Aralia elata	3 × 2m/10 × 6ft	Single upright stem bears large, divided leaves; in summer plumes of white flowers	Dramatic for back of the border
Corokia cotoneaster (wire netting bush)	0.6 × 1m/2 × 3ft	The common name says it all!	Needs acid soil and warm spot
Corylus avellana 'Contorta' (corkscrew hazel)	3 × 3m/10 × 10ft	Twisted branches	Makes unusual winter feature at back of border; remove straight-stemmed suckers from base
Cotoneaster horizontalis	1 × 3m/3 × 10ft	'Fish-bone' branches with small dark green leaves and red berries in autumn	Tolerant
Genista aetnensis	5 × 5m/16 × 16ft	Elegant and graceful small tree with minute leaves; yellow flowers in early summer	Dislikes damp soil and cold areas
Griselinia littoralis	5 × 5m/16 × 16ft	Shrub or small tree with thick, glossy leaves on upward-sweeping branches	Dislikes cold areas

A border is just not about flowers, but involves leaves, seedheads and plant form, too.

Griselinia littoralis, a shrub or small tree with attractively upward-sweeping branches. Many trees and shrubs can be made to grow formally by means of clipping – yew, box and bay are among the most widely seen examples.

Formal shapes should not be restricted to formal borders. A strong, formal shape has a remarkable ability to transform a border. An informal, almost wild border will look completely different if it includes a strong geometrical shape, like columnar or pyramidal clipped yew. It makes the informality look more intentional, and the contrast between the two is stimulating. Such strong, clear shapes, are also useful for helping to develop a sense of unity if they are repeated several times in a border (see pages 48–54).

Formal shapes can also look effective in borders near buildings, especially if the architecture is of a quality that needs some reference to it in the surroundings. Shrubs or trees trained as standards add an atmosphere of classical or Mediterranean formality, especially if several are spaced at regular intervals. In too informal a border though, they might seem overwhelmed and irrelevant.

Informal plant shapes that are notably pleasing tend to be so because they look elegant or unusual or because they have a certain sculptural quality. Layered foliage, like that of the shrub *Viburnum*

Plant shapes

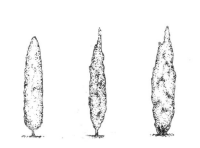

Columnar: tall, thin shapes that draw the eye up to the heavens have a particular use in the garden. Their ability to combine the virtue of height with the necessity of space saving makes them invaluable (see pages 76–9). Although there are few really good columnar plants, it is possible to clip yew and many cypress-type trees into this shape.

Upright growth: many plants, chiefly shrubs but also some herbaceous perennials, have a habit of growth that is strongly vertical, although without the formality and neatness of columnar growers. They give a sense of the vertical, which is a welcome change

to the more amorphous, clumpy nature of most border plants. Usually it is the stems that create the upright sensation, and in the case of some of the shrubs it is more marked in winter when the plants are leafless. Their natural place seems to be at the back of the border or dotted around the larger open border, where there should not be too much in front to obscure them.

Pyramids and cones: taking up more space than a column, there are few plants that naturally adopt this habit of growth. Dwarf spruces and firs form neat Christmas-tree shapes, and many other dwarf conifers have an approximate cone shape. It is, however, an easy shape to achieve by clipping, which can be used on a very wide range of shrubs or trees.

Geometric shapes: all products of the clipper's art, these can be fun. It is surprisingly easy to make cubes and other geometrical shapes from shrubs by a kind of simple topiary, which may be used to give a formal touch to a border or, if used asymmetrically, a more imaginatively modernistic one. Any species with relatively close twiggy growth is suitable, although small specimens are best made with traditional topiary material, like yew or box. All such geometrical shapes are much appreciated in the winter.

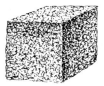

Rounded: a few dwarf shrubs naturally form entertainingly round shapes, which look good when they are allowed to billow over low walls. The most perfect and long-lasting balls are made by certain hebes – *H. cupressoides* 'Boughton Dome', for example. Many Mediterranean shrubs, like santolina and sage, also do this, although less perfectly, needing clipping after flowering. Such rounded, hummocky plants are ideal for the front of the border, particularly where the border is fronted by a hard surface with a straight line that needs breaking up.

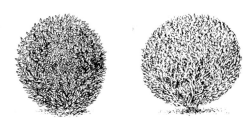

Elegant: very much in the eye of the beholder, elegant plants are both graceful and have a sense of the sculptural. The airy growths of some grasses and perennials add a light touch to the border, especially if rather dumpy or low forms predominate. Larger shrubby plants with graceful growth are good as counterbalances to their more solid neighbours. The main aspect of elegant plants, however, is that they can be appreciated only when they are not crowded. Like a good dancer, these plants need some space around them if their virtues are to be seen.

Spreading: plants that form low, spreading shapes, especially if they are layered rather than just being a carpet of growth, are useful as filler plants for the front of the border, particularly in situations where there is a hard surface such as a path in front of the border. Their horizontal nature provides a counterbalance to vertical, upright lines.

Arching: many grasses and some perennials and shrubs adopt this habit, although it is a late season development for the perennials and shrubs. The weight of flowers and seedheads causes the stems to bend outwards gracefully. Useful for autumn elegance, a good arching plant needs space to be appreciated.

Vase shapes: many ferns adopt a distinct vase shape, which is one of the few stronger shapes to be seen among shade-loving plants. If a border in shade seems to be dominated by low and creeping forms, the addition of a few taller ferns with this habit can make all the difference.

Weeping or pendent: true weeping trees or shrubs are not really natural, but chance mutations have been selected and propagated for the garden. Smaller varieties do have great structural potential in the border, where they are often more of a feature in winter and early spring.

plicatum or of the branches of dwarf spruces, looks elegant to many and adds a horizontal dimension. The 'fish-bone' pattern of growth of the shrub *Cotoneaster horizontalis* is another example of informal yet ordered growth that always adds interest to a border. More extreme are shrubs or small trees with contorted growth like the well-known corkscrew hazel (*Corylus avellana* 'Contorta'). In winter such plants add a major source of interest to any border.

Trees and shrubs are the main source of shape in the garden, their permanence adding a sense of stability through time, just as their shape gives stability to the appearance of the border. But many perennials, and especially ornamental grasses, have interesting and beautiful shapes, which, of course, change rapidly through the year. Some grasses are sternly upright, but most are attractive through having a more informally graceful quality. Late summer and autumn are the best time to appreciate these plants, and many remain tidy and sufficiently good-looking to be worth looking at even in the earlier part of winter.

While many grasses form pleasing hummocky shapes, with soft-textured flower- and seedheads in contrast to more dynamic and stronger plant forms, some have a more distinctive upright and somewhat bamboo-like shape, and others form low-level, rosette-based growths. Some of the most delightful grasses, notably *Stipa gigantea*, send out sprays of seedheads on long airy stems, and it is possible to see 'through' them, so that the plants beyond are visible through a haze. True bamboos are invariably graceful in appearance and most useful in providing evergreen shrub-like bulk but with an elegant upright habit. They are rarely used in borders, which is a shame as they have so much to contribute. The invasive, thuggish habits of some bamboos have

The distinctive shape of their flowerheads makes kniphofias among the most useful of summer border plants.

given a bad name to them all, but most, in fact, do not spread particularly vigorously.

Combining rounded plants with upright ones and spreading plants with conical ones, all interspersed with more amorphously shaped plants, is the best recipe for interest and avoids both overstimulation and boredom. Just how much contrast is introduced into a border is a matter of personal taste: some people thrive on a lot, others prefer just enough to provide interest. Those who like it can use a high proportion of plants with clear shapes, juxtapose them and include some with strong, dynamic shapes like the spiky rosettes of yuccas.

Combining shapes

Harmonious contrast results from balancing a variety of plant shapes.

The bringing together of several dramatically shaped plants or those with large or spiky foliage is often unsuccessful. It strikes many as a jumble of competing forms.

The use of one dramatic plant – a yucca, for example – can make all the difference to a border of less well-defined shapes. It will make a good focal point or eye-catcher.

Repeating a clear shape at regular intervals adds a strong sense of regularity to a border, however 'wild' the rest of the planting may be. Even irregularly placed repeating elements perform a similar function.

Those who do not like such strong or dramatic contrasts can work with a more restricted selection of plant shapes.

Ultimately, mixing shapes comes down to a combination of upright and lower spreading forms. Not only does a border composed entirely of upright forms look unsatisfying but it is impractical too: the ground remains bare, open to weed infestation and excessive drying. A border of low, clumpy forms will not suffer from these problems, but it will seem insipid. Many of the plants that are used as filler plants (see page 43) will be of the low-growing kind, interweaving between more upright and visually arresting ones.

Blue flowers and yellow foliage –
Spiraea japonica 'Goldflame' with a geranium – make
an effective contrast.

Plants with dramatic foliage

	HEIGHT × SPREAD	FLOWERS AND FOLIAGE	NOTES
Fatsia japonica	3 × 3m/10 × 10ft	Shrub with large, glossy leaves	Good as centrepiece of border in light shade; dislikes winds
Melianthus major	1.2 × 1m/4 × 3ft (if treated as herbaceous perennial)	Stunning divided, silver leaves	Must have moist, but well-drained hot spot and good winter protection
Musa basjoo (Japanese banana)	2 × 0.6m/6 × 2ft	Exotic-looking, large, green leaves	Almost hardy; stems must be wrapped in insulating material over winter
Paulownia tomentosa	3 × 2m/10 × 6ft	Cut down every year to give the best sized leaves	Dramatic centrepiece to a border; dislikes extreme cold
Phormium tenax	2 × 2.5m/6 × 8ft	Bronze, sword-shaped leaves in a large rosette	Need space and, preferably, a mild, moist climate
Yucca filamentosa	2 × 3m/6 × 10ft (eventually)	Dramatic, spiky plant	Makes good focal point in a border; needs full sun and good drainage

Damp soil provides the perfect conditions for dramatic foliage –
Gunnera tinctoria with *Hosta sieboldiana* and the fern *Dryopteris filix-mas*.

FOLIAGE

The beauty of leaves is often overlooked, yet their season is much longer than that of flowers, and this makes them useful for situations where a long season of interest is important, such as in small borders in prominent places or in shady situations where the number of flowering plants that can be grown is limited by lack of light. But it should not merely be necessity that makes us look at foliage.

Leaves need to be appreciated on several levels; one is colour, which is dealt with in the section on colour (see pages 98–114), another is the appearance of leaves from a distance, their contribution to the visual texture of a border as a whole (see page 91), and the other is what they look like close up.

This last quality of foliage – its appearance when

seen near to — really makes a contribution to the border as a whole only in small borders. Situations that are confined but important — such as court-yards, the surroundings of a door or other entrance or a frequently walked but narrow pathway — are ideal for a leaf-dominated mini-border, especially if the area is shaded. Woodland plants often have inter-esting foliage, which is frequently also evergreen. Putting together a collection of shade-loving foliage plants for a lightly shaded or fully shaded area is remarkably easy and rewarding, because there is enormous scope for developing contrasts between different leaf shapes, sizes, colours and textures, especially if imaginative use of ferns is made so that their filigree delicacy is allowed to create contrasts with the flat, dark glossiness of many flowering shade-lovers.

When it comes to considering foliage in a broader context and the ways it can be used in a mixed border to maximum effect, it is helpful to think of two broad categories: bold strong shapes that imme-diately grab the attention and more retiring foliage, which is usually composed of smaller, more finely textured leaves.

The first category includes many perennials with large or bold foliage that gives them a lush or even exotic look, perhaps the ultimate example being the moisture-loving giant rhubarb (*Gunnera manicata*). Some shrubs have distinct, large foliage too, but they are less common. The possibilities of using dramatic foliage is greater in warmer areas, where a wider range of plants can be grown, but a lot are, never-theless, hardy, although they must nearly always be grown out of the wind, which can do terrible damage to large leaves, and many (chiefly the perennials) grow best in moist and fertile soil.

Plants with bold foliage are wonderful for creating a dramatic planting or for cultivating a semi-tropical look, when several can be included in a border. Just the occasional specimen of such a plant can really add character to a border, making a striking visual statement that is largely indepen-dent of any colour scheme. If the exotic look is wanted, a whole border could be composed with such plants, although the result may be too visu-ally fussy for many people. It is worth bearing in mind that it might be difficult to fit flowering plants into such a border, for they could end up looking tame and a bit overwhelmed. Bold, exotic-looking flowers would be best, even if many suitable con-tenders are half-hardy, like cannas and dahlias.

One point to bear in mind with bold, or indeed with glossy, foliage is that because, like a bright colour, it draws attention to itself it foreshortens perspective. Therefore, if it is used at the end of a border (when viewed from the most usual point), the border may appear shorter than it really is. Small and/or matt foliage has the opposite effect, because it is 'retiring', making itself and its surroundings look further away. This effect is enhanced by the size of foliage. Large-leaved plants, even if they are soft to look at, stand out, whereas small ones do not. As we have already noted, too much dramatic foliage in one place can be tiring to the eye, like a group of small children all competing for attention. Rela-tively undistinguished foliage is useful if you want to emphasize flowers in the border and perhaps mini-mize competition for attention. Probably the most useful for this kind of situation are plants that have small, matt leaves.

Canna 'Wyoming' is one of several exotic-looking half-hardy foliage plants that can be used in summer borders. In winter it will need to be well insulated or removed under cover.

Leaf shapes

Large: looks grand and exotic, but can be overwhelming and out of place in the smaller border. The best place to make a feature out of large leaves is a sheltered place on a moist soil.

Round, heart-shaped: among perennials, this type of leaf can often be found on moisture-loving plants. It makes plants look attractively lush, but can get monotonous if overdone. These leaves tend to be found on clump-forming, low-level perennials.

Pinnate: the name given to multiple leaves, when leaflets grow out of a central stem. Such leaves are often a good contrast to other foliage, and large pinnate leaves can look magnificent and rather tropical. Pinnate leaves of distinction are nearly always on shrubs, and the best ones are on trees.

Palmate: the name palmate applies when leaflets come out from a central point at the tip of a stem. Smaller palmate leaves often look rather elegant; larger ones look exotic. Such leaves are seen on only a limited number of shrubs and perennials.

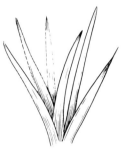

Fern-like or feathery: such leaves are essentially pinnate but with further and finer divisions; alternatively, they are just a very finely divided pinnate leaf. They are valuable for contrast with coarser textured leaves and very often beautiful in their own right, but too many together and the border can look out of focus. Such leaves are almost entirely a feature of ferns and perennials rather than of shrubs.

Strap-, sword-like and other linear leaves: these leaves are essential for providing contrast with other types of leaves, especially since in many cases – irises, for example – they are upright or arching. Although, to most eyes, they do not look 'right' when placed in serried ranks, when they are interspersed through a border they create a vital 'change of pace'.

Grassy: these leaves are similar to strap-like leaves but finer. The soft texture they provide looks good next to coarser foliage. Whether different species look good next to each other is a matter of opinion: many people feel they definitely do not.

Bamboo-like: linear foliage spaced out on upright stems often looks very graceful, especially if the stems arch outwards. Such leaves bring introduce a touch of delicacy to the border. Apart from bamboos themselves, a few shrubs have a similar effect.

Spiky: larger versions of strap-like leaves, these are wonderful bringing an 'exclamation mark' emphasis to the border. They can, however, look very restless or even aggressive if there are too many. These leaves often occur on plants from warm or dry climates and so are good for creating an exotic border in areas of summer drought.

TEXTURE

Foliage gives plants a visual texture. It may be either hard and glossy, like shiny laurel leaves, or soft and matt, like the leaves of a hardy fuchsia. There are a few plants with foliage that is so finely textured that it is quite exceptional and thus of considerable use in the border. Plants with masses of small, neat leaves – jasmine, for instance – are a restful backdrop for stronger shapes. Many low, bushy plants, such as santolina or lavender, have such small leaves that they are recognizable only close up, and plants such as these are a good contrast with larger leaves or definitive stem shapes. The herb fennel is a good example of a plant with an exceptional texture: the mass of dark, finely divided leaves, which are impossible to make out any detail, forms almost a visual 'black hole' in the border. It seems to work especially well when it is planted next to strong colours.

Shade offers perhaps the best place to play with texture. A shady border can include many attractive foliage shapes, and ferns in particular offer a huge variety of texture from the extremely fine to the hardy and shiny, like the hart's tongue fern, *Asplenium* (formerly *Phyllitis*) *scolopendrium*.

ARTEFACTS

Statues, containers, bird-baths, sundials and sculptures – all these have a place in gardens as well as plants. But in the border? Artefacts are usually positioned in the garden much as specimen plants might be, on their own in splendid isolation. Whether they are placed in a border is, like all matters of taste, entirely a personal decision. Some artefacts might suffer by being concealed or 'lost' among the burgeoning growth of a mixed border, but others might well benefit from this unusual positioning. The appeal of artefacts is different from that of plants, and the two might be too divergent. If they are to

Evergreens

Not all evergreens are dark green; there are many other colours, notably blue-grey, golden-yellow and silver, gold and cream variegation. It also helps to think of certain perennials and grasses as being evergreen. This chart summarizes the possibilities.

TYPE OF PLANT	CHARACTERISTICS OF FOLIAGE	USE IN BORDER	AVAILABILITY	EXAMPLES
Shrubs with dark foliage	Usually dark, often glossy	Background for light foliage and flowers; something green in winter	Larger number of varieties	*Buxus sempervirens; Ilex* species; *Prunus laurocerasus; P. lusitanicus;* rhododendrons; conifers; bamboos
Shrubs with gold variegation	Splashes of yellow or gold on leaves, sometimes covering almost all of leaf surface	Bring a feeling of sunshine to the border in winter	Good range of possibilities	*Elaeagnus pungens* 'Maculata'; variegated varieties of *Euonymus* and *Ilex*
Shrubs with silver variegation or silver-grey foliage	Splashes of silver or cream on leaves, sometimes covering almost all of leaf surface or silver-grey foliage	Create a sensation of light, especially in shade; useful for 'cooling' bright flowers	Somewhat wider range than gold	Varieties of *Brachyglottis, Euonymus, Hebe, Ilex, Lavandula* and *Phlomis; Convolvulus cneorum*
Climbers with evergreen foliage	Most are glossy and dark; some with gold or silver variegation	Winter background for a border if grown on wall or fence	Apart from ivies, of which there are many, the selection is limited	*Clematis armandii; Hedera* (ivies) and *Trachelospermum* species
Perennials	Most are dark green and glossy; some have silver variation	Bring a feeling of life to shadier corners too small for evergreen shrubs	Not a great many varieties, but still a lot of scope	*Achillea, Ajuga, Helleborus, Kniphofia Pulmonaria* and *Vinca* species; *Stachys olympica*
Ferns	Dark leaves, usually relatively undivided for ferns	Low-level winter green; tend to be good in dry shade	Limited selection and can be hard to find	*Asplenium scolopendrium; Dryopteris filix-mas* (semi-evergreen); *Polystichum acrostichoides*
Grasses and sedges with yellow, red, bronze or variegated foliage	Silver or gold banding on leaves or, more usually, a uniform colour	Invaluable for winter colour at lower levels	Rapidly increasing in range and availability	*Carex, Elymus, Festuca* and *Luzula* species

work well together they must complement each other and not compete for attention.

One great argument in favour of having artefacts in borders is that they are usually permanent. They will be there come rain or shine, summer or winter, which is more than we can say for many plants. Indeed, there is no reason why you should not have ornamental structures in the border that are visible only in winter.

Recent years have seen a great increase in the range and number of garden artefacts that are designed to be used with plants and, often in fact, to be intimately involved with them, including trellis, obelisks, archways and pillars. Many of these items are designed to be used with climbers or lax shrubs like tall roses. Obelisks are a good example of an artefact that is primarily practical (as a support for small climbers) but that looks attractive in its own right in winter when the climber has died down. Archways and pergolas may be decoratively

Textures of seedhead, leaf and flower: alliums combine with *Anemone* × *hybrida* and silver *Senecio viravira.*

Plants with interesting texture

	HEIGHT × SPREAD	FLOWERS AND FOLIAGE	NOTES
Hebe cupressoides 'Boughton Dome'	80 × 80cm/32 × 32in	Masses of tiny twigs set with scale-like leaves	Dwarf shrub forming perfect dome; many other similar varieties
Hydrangea sargentiana	2.5 × 3m/8 × 10ft	Huge, dark, hairy leaves on upright stems; mauve flowerheads	Good in shade at the back of the border
Magnolia grandiflora	To 30m/98ft (but can be kept clipped)	Fine yellowish, glossy leaves and huge white flowers in late summer	Avoid windy or exposed sites
Phlomis fruticosa	70 × 70cm/28 × 28in	Dark leaves with a matt texture; golden-yellow flowers in early summer	Good for front of border; dislikes winter damp and extreme cold
Tamarix tetrandra	3 × 3m/10 × 10ft	Soft, hazy looking foliage with clouds of pink flowers in late summer	Needs full sun

Sculpture can be figurative (left), while metal plant supports (above) can double as abstract art.

designed, too, so that they are not simply functional. Trellis, once a purely utilitarian product, is now available in many ornamental forms, and it may be used as a backdrop for planting or as a screen that can also be used for supporting plants.

Items that were once regarded as functional necessities, to be hidden as quickly as possible, are now becoming garden ornaments in their own right. The humble bean pole, multiplied to form a tent- or wigwam-like structure, has been replaced in many gardens by highly fashionable but eminently practical structures that do the same trick, such as

willow supports for sweet peas (or beans – the flowers are pretty) or ornamental cages.

The most successful artefact and border combinations are often those that involve objects made from plant-derived materials – bamboo, willow and the like – or that make a reference to the plant world. Terracotta, which brings to mind the colour of the soil, or something made from local stone, which relates to the natural surroundings of the garden, can link the garden border to a wider environment.

Containers are sometimes combined with borders. Classical urns spilling pelargoniums and

Rustic 'wigwams' or twigs to support sweet peas are attractive in their own right.
Digitalis lutea blooms at front right and *Monarda* 'Cambridge Scarlet' at left.

bedding or perhaps containing an exotic succulent like an agave, make a fine centrepiece or cornerpiece for a border. Growing plants in containers and putting them in or alongside the border is a way of including plants that require conditions different from those prevailing in the border. A camellia in a wooden barrel that is full of the humus-rich, lime-free compost in which it thrives can be combined with roses and perennials on an alkaline clay and

will give us something to look at in early spring, long before the main interest of the border has got going.

If you would like to create a particular ambience within the garden, it may be possible to use plants and ornamental artefacts together. For example, a hint of the Far East can be developed by using bamboos and tree peonies and then reinforced by the inclusion of a Japanese-style lantern.

7

Colour

THE SUBJECT OF COLOUR causes people more problems than anything else. It leads otherwise reasonable people to make sweeping and dogmatic statements; and it make others, normally bold, shy of doing anything counter to what they perceive to be the ruling fashion. Colour, for most gardeners, is what the border is all about, and it is certainly the place in the garden where it is impossible not to mix colours. As far as most readers of this book are concerned, the key question in creating a border is how to get the colour 'right'.

Despite the vast number of words that have been written on the subject, there is no such thing as 'good' or 'bad' colour combinations. There are reasons, scientific and objective, why some colours and combinations of colours evoke certain feelings in people, but this is not to say that particular colour combinations are inherently or objectively better than others. The appreciation of colour is subjective and is strongly affected by culture, taste and fashion. It is also, there can be no doubt, largely about what people think they ought to like.

Making a garden is an individual, personal process. It is your garden, and you should include in it what you want, not what you feel you ought to like. Have the courage of your convictions, and if you want a magenta and orange border, you should ignore whatever warnings I may deliver and go ahead and plant it.

Although flower colour is the overwhelming focus for most gardeners, foliage colour is important, too, simply because there are so many leaves that are anything but green. There are purple and yellow hued plants, and leaves with silver, cream

White borders are cool and refreshing.
Tulipa 'White Dream' and *T.* 'Mount Tacoma' mingle
with *Omphalodes linifolia.*

Colour combinations

The main characteristics of each of the main flower and foliage colours are described, followed by a selection of two colour combinations, together with suggestions for adding third colours. These are divided into three:

• Level 1 combinations are easy, with a wide variety of plants available and little opportunity to create anything garish that might offend anyone.

• Level 2 combinations need a bit more thought and confidence in handling colour. Give them a try, but you might find yourself doing some rearranging at the end of the season. Success here will bring accolades from gardening neighbours.

• Level 3 combinations are definitely daring or dangerous. Passers-by may reach for their sunglasses, but if you like the results, stick with it!

REDS
• Hot
• Dark (first to disappear in the evening)
• Look best in strong sun
• Limited range of plants

ORANGES
• Hot
• Fierce
• Dominant, eye-catching
• Limited range of plants

RED-BROWNS/RUSSETS
• Warm
• Autumnal look
• Look best in low evening light
• Reasonable range of plants if foliage is included

YELLOWS
• Cheerful in spring
• Bright, possibly fierce in summer
• Add light to dark colours and dark places
• Very wide range of plants

YELLOW-GREENS
• Light
• Good foil for bright colours
• Good buffer between strong colours
• Effective in shade
• Wide range of plants with this foliage, fewer with flowers

SOFT PINKS
• Soothing and calming
• Often tinged with blue or violet
• Very wide range of plants

MAGENTAS AND STRONG PINKS
• Aggressive, attention seeking
• Shorten perspective (i.e., magenta flowers appear to be closer than they really are)
• Limited range of plants in strong magenta

BLUES
• The coolest colour
• Distant, lengthening perspective (making them appear further away)
• Look best in shade
• Last colour (apart from white) to disappear in the evening
• Wide range of plants (as purple-blue)

VIOLET AND PURPLES/MAUVES
• Cool
• Distant (i.e., appear to be further away than they are)
• Dark
• Very wide range of plants
• Don't forget purple foliage

DEEP PURPLE, MAROONS, 'BLACK'
• Surreal
• Dark, sombre
• Unusual
• Limited range of plants

WHITES AND CREAMS
• Cool
• Light
• Good in shade
• Make even small flowers stand out
• The best buffer colours
• Very wide range of plants

SILVER-GREYS
• Cool
• Light
• Good foil for other colour (apart from yellows)
• Good buffer between strong colours
• Wide range of plants with silver or grey foliage

L E V E L   1

RED + YELLOW
- Hot
- Classic summer combination
- Yellow lightens the reds
- Now add orange

RED-BROWN + YELLOW
- Autumnal
- Warm
- Very effective and harmonious
- Now add some deeper reds

SILVER + PINK
- Cool and tasteful
- Easy to make a good associations
- Now add pale blues and lavender shades

WHITE + PINK
- Relaxing
- Possibly too sugary for some
- Easy to do
- Now add blues and purples to create more variety

WHITE + BLUE
- Cool, refreshing
- Very good in shade and the evening

SILVER + BLUE
- Very cool
- Now add some pink for a little more warmth

L E V E L   2

YELLOW + PURPLE
- A safe contrast
- Colours enhance each other
- Purple flowers against foliage
- Now add some blues

YELLOW + BLUE
- An 'easy' contrast
- The colour enhance each other
- A good all-season combination

MAGENTA + YELLOW-GREEN
or MAGENTA + BLUE
- Magenta calmed down by the other colours
- Magenta enhances the paler colours
- Very effective as a highlight

MAGENTA + DARK PURPLE
- Very dark
- Moody
- Best as a sophisticated highlight
- Limited plant availability

YELLOW-GREEN + BLUE
- Sophisticated
- Harmonious
- Works well in spring
- Now add the occasional pink for variety

SILVER + DARK PURPLE
- Unusual and sophisticated
- Limited possibilities

BLUE + VIOLET
- Easy
- Dark – can be sombre
- Now add white – or pink – to lighten

SILVER + VIOLET
- Startling and dynamic
- Livens up the purples

WHITE + VIOLET
- Energetic but cool
- The white brightens the darkness of the purples
- Now add blues, too

L E V E L   3

RED + PINK
- Not always successful; results can be dull
- Add white as a buffer
- Now try adding blue

RED + BLUE
- Striking but lacks the light touch
- Add white as a buffer; its light transforms the association

PINK + YELLOW
- Rarely successful
- Try adding blue

BLUE + ORANGE
- Very striking
- Only for the daring
- Best if blues outnumber oranges

ORANGE + MAGENTA
- A shocker, but less so in strong sunlight or low autumn light
- Best as small planting
- If you've gone this far, now add scarlet

and gold variegation. There are also the brightly coloured barks and twigs of certain shrubs and small trees to consider for the border, and these are particularly appreciated in winter.

SEASON AND CLIMATE

Choosing plant colours is not like choosing emulsion paint for home decorating; there is not an almost infinite number of choices available for every situation. Particular colours may be limited at certain times of year, effectively restricting some colour schemes.

Some colours do seem to predominate at specific times of year, and these colours may indeed suggest themselves as seasonal colour schemes. Spring is especially good for variations on yellow and intense blues, daffodils and bluebells (*Hyacinthoides non-scripta*) respectively being the first two that come to mind. There are plenty of other strong colours at this time as well, notably scarlet and bright pink tulips and the myriad shades of modern polyanthus varieties. Yet the relatively low light levels of spring seem to ensure that all these colours work well together, and perhaps the fact that we have been starved of colour during winter makes us more accepting of combinations of bright colours.

Early summer seems to be the time for pinks and blues, with shrub roses setting the tone. Such pastel colour schemes are easy at this time, but they work best in climates with grey skies when the subtle variations in pink and mauve can be appreciated. Late summer and autumn is for deep reds, yellows and purples. There is a definite tendency for bird-pollinated subtropical plants to feature deep red, and this is when they are usually at their best. Yellow and purple combinations are particularly effective, and as the light levels get lower there are some really 'shocking' red, magenta and yellow combinations

that become not only possible but more acceptable, as autumn leaf colours mix with varieties of aster, chrysanthemum and rudbeckia.

Visits to gardens that are open to the public and to flower shows are an excellent way of appreciating these seasonal colour variations. Take a pencil and paper and make a note of any particular combinations or themes that you like or that might be especially suitable for your border.

COLOUR STRATEGIES

Gardeners work with colour in various ways, and before you get too involved with your new border and too committed to one plan, it might be helpful to consider the broad strategies that you might adopt.

- **Single colour schemes:** this is easy and guaranteed to be effective (as long as you are not too fussy and limit your choices too narrowly).
- **Related colour schemes:** choosing a number of colours that work together well is a bit more of a challenge, but the self-imposed limits ensure that the 'colour clashes' that so many fear will be unlikely.
- **Contrasting colour schemes:** this scheme, which is a bit more daring, involves choosing colours that are 'opposite' on the colour wheel and that make a startling combination together. Extremely effective when done well, it takes skill.
- **Neutral schemes:** colour may not interest you as much as form and texture, or you may just love the plants for themselves, and if this is so, you will use criteria other than colour in selecting the plants, just being careful that juxtaposed colours do not cause too much discord.
- **Colour riot:** you love colour, lots of it and lots of different shades and regard people who are worried about colour clashes as being highly strung. Go for it!

Single-colour Borders

Exploring the possibilities of one colour is an easy way to create a border and makes it into an ongoing project. You will find yourself keeping an eye out for flowers in your preferred colour wherever you go, constantly making additions and improvements to your list. And you will not just be looking for flowers, because every year more and more plant varieties with coloured foliage appear on the market, including varieties with variegated leaves as well as those whose leaves are flushed red, purple, bronze or yellow.

White borders are an easy and wonderfully soothing introduction to the single colour idea. Once you start looking, you will quickly realize just how few true pure white flowers there are. There is an enormous range of off-white blooms though, as practically every plant seems to have a white-flowered form, giving you lots of scope on all soil types and

in all situations and opportunities for a long season of interest. Silver-grey and white- or cream-variegated foliage goes wonderfully with white flowers and, of course, gives the border a much longer season, and if evergreens are used, the theme can be made to last all year round.

Red borders (see pages 107–9 on hot colour borders) can be oppressive. Red is a dark colour, especially when it is combined with purple or red foliage, which is often done. The range of plants is somewhat limited, too. Summer, especially late summer, will see abundant plants, but the rest of the year may be a bit sparse. Only a little yellow, either as flowers or as golden-splashed or yellow-hued foliage, can make all the difference, helping to create a much lighter composition.

Yellow gives you plenty of opportunity, and there is a seemingly endless selection of yellow flowers

Best whites

	HEIGHT × SPREAD	FLOWERS AND FOLIAGE	NOTES
Bergenia 'Silberlicht'	30 × 50cm/1ft × 1ft 8in	Flowers early; evergreen foliage	Grows in sun or light shade; tolerant
Epilobium angustifolium var. *album*	1.2 × 0.5m/4ft × 1ft 8in	Spikes of flower in late summer	Tolerant; not invasive
Hebe 'White Gem'	2 × 2m/6 × 6ft	Dense spikes of white flowers in midsummer; evergreen foliage	Dislikes severe cold
Libertia grandiflora	80 × 60cm/2ft 8in × 2ft	Clump-forming perennial with iris-like leaves; flowers in mid- to late summer	Dislikes extreme cold
Rosa 'Iceberg'	1 × 0.8m/3ft × 2ft 8in	Double flowers and apple-like scent throughout summer	
Spiraea nipponica 'Snowmound	2 × 2m/6 × 6ft	Shrub with masses of white flowers in early summer	Tolerant

and a wide variety of yellow or gold foliage. In fact, you will be spoilt for choice from spring to early autumn. The results will be cheerful and bright, and quite insufferable for visitors who hate yellow flowers – and a lot of people do. Golden-variegated evergreen foliage is especially valued for bringing sunshine to winter days.

Planting a blue border is rather a tall order. Connoisseurs of this colour will appreciate that there are hardly any blue flowers, only mauve and purple ones. Very few 'blue' flowers contain no red pigment. Blue-mauve-purple borders are practically unknown in my experience, despite there being plenty of material from spring to late autumn, so, if you want to start a trend ... The results might be rather dark, however, so try blending in white and perhaps the occasional plant with yellow-hued foliage.

Critics of 'one-colour gardening' always point to a deadness that can result. Too much of the same thing can lead to a kind of 'boredom' of the retina. Adding just a few plants of another colour can make all the difference, offering the eye some contrast. Blue works well with yellow and with red. Coloured foliage is especially useful in the blue border because it has a longer season than flowers and because it is usually more subtle.

Related Colour Borders

Borders planned on the basis of related colours take the concept of the single-colour border a stage further, putting together two or more colours that look good and exploring the potential variations and their relationships with each other. Because colours fall approximately into two camps, hot and cool/pastel, we usually see a variation on one of these two themes.

Best reds

	HEIGHT × SPREAD	FLOWERS AND FOLIAGE	NOTES
Chaenomeles × superba 'Rowallane'	1.2 × 2m/4 × 6ft	Sprawling shrub with early scarlet flowers	Does best in sun
Crinodendron hookerianum (Chile lantern tree)	3 × 2.5m/10 × 8ft	Upright shrub with dark red 'Chinese lanterns' in early summer; dark evergreen leaves	Dislikes cold and lime
Potentilla atrosanguinea	40 × 70cm/16 × 28in	Sprawling perennial with dark red flowers in midsummer	Needs sun
Rhododendron 'Elizabeth'	1.5 × 1.5m/5 × 5ft	Tubular scarlet flowers in late spring; neat foliage	Dislikes lime and drought
Salvia rutilans	1 × 1m/3 × 3ft	Tubular scarlet flowers in late summer; pineapple-scented foliage	Half-hardy
Tropaeolum speciosum (nasturtium)	3m/10ft (climber)	Perennial with scarlet flowers in late summer	Looks good on a dark hedge; does best in mild, moist climates in lime-free soil

Best yellows

	Height × spread	Flowers and foliage	Notes
Cytisus × praecox 'Allgold'	1.2 × 1.2m/4 × 4ft	Upright shrub with profuse golden flowers in late spring	Does best in sun
Forsythia × intermedia 'Spectabilis'	3 × 3m/10 × 10ft	Masses of rich yellow flowers early in year	Untidy habit; best in large borders; tolerant
Fremontodendron californicum	3 × 2m/10 × 6ft	Large, rich yellow flowers in summer; evergreen foliage	Usually grown on warm wall; dislikes damp cold and wind
Potentilla fruticosa 'Vilmoriniana'	1.5 × 1m/5 × 3ft	Shrub with pale yellow flowers throughout summer	Needs sun
Rudbeckia fulgida var. *sullivantii* 'Goldsturm'	50 × 60cm/20 × 24in	Yellow daisies with dark centres in late summer to early autumn	Compact habit
Verbascum chaixii 'Gainsborough'	1.2 × 0.4m/4 ft × 1ft 4in	Primrose-yellow flowers on a narrow spike in summer	Short lived but self-seeds

Best true blues

	Height × spread	Flowers and foliage	Notes
Anchusa azurea	50 × 60cm/20 × 24in	Deep blue flowers in early summer	Needs sun
Ceanothus impressus	1.5 × 3m/5 × 10ft	Sprawling shrub with profuse blue flowers in early summer	Does best on poor, dry soils in full sun
Corydalis flexuosa	15 × 30cm/6 × 12in	Deep electric blue flowers in spring	Dies down in summer; needs a moist, lightly shaded site
Omphalodes cappadocica	15 × 30cm/6 × 12in	Bright blue flowers in late spring	Spreading perennial; needs light shade
Salvia patens	40 × 50cm/16 × 20in	Deep blue flowers in late summer	Half-hardy
Symphytum caucasicum	60 × 90cm/2 × 3ft	Bright blue pendent flowers above hairy green leaves	Looks good in wild garden; rampant

ABOVE: *Allium christophii* and *Geranium × magnificum*
are a startling combination in early summer
LEFT: Silver or grey foliage can be used to 'cool' strong
colour combinations, such as this sedum and aster.

'Hot' Borders

A border falls into this category when it uses red, oranges and yellows, the colours that we know psychologically as 'hot'. The results may be spectacular, but they are not restful to the eye. Not surprisingly, this is very much a summer-style of border, for not only does mid- to late summer offer the widest range of flowers in these colours but the colours, especially red, look best in strong light.

A hot border will have to rely on perennials for the bulk of its effect, because few hardy shrubs have

Pyrethrum, crocosmia and penstemon varieties blaze away in a sunny border in
late summer. The variegated aralia affords some respite from the red.

Best bright pinks and magentas

	HEIGHT × SPREAD	FLOWERS AND FOLIAGE	NOTES
Erodium manescavii	30 × 30cm/1 × 1ft	Flowers throughout summer	Grows in sun or light shade
Geranium psilostemon	1 × 1m/3 × 3ft	Dark-eyed flowers in early summer with a second flush later	Grows in sun or light shade
Lychnis coronaria	80 × 20cm/32 × 8in	Silver leaves; dark magenta flowers in late summer	Short lived but self-seeds; needs sun
Lythrum salicaria; L. virgatum	1 × 0.4m/3ft × 1ft 4in	Spikes of flowers in midsummer	Does best in sun in moist soil
Rosa 'Zéphirine Drouhin'	2.5 × 2m/8 × 6ft	Deep pink flowers all summer	Best grown as a climber

flowers in these colours. There are many yellow perennials, but good oranges and reds are not so easy to find. Fortunately, there are a lot of fine hardy and half-hardy annuals that provide all three colours, with some of the best reds coming from late-flowering tender plants. A hot border will thus look best late in the season. Foliage as well as flower can contribute to a hot border. Gold-variegated, yellow-tinted and purple- and red-flushed foliage can all play a part. There is a wide range of shrubs and perennials with coloured foliage, and the shrubs make a useful background for the flower colours.

If all this seems a bit restive, there are a couple of options for 'cooling it down'. One is by introducing the occasional splash of grey foliage; another is the complementary effect of fresh green leaves on scarlet, a powerful but refreshing combination.

Pastel Borders

Borders based on pinks, blues and mauves, whites and silver have become one of the most popular of

Best blue-purples

	HEIGHT × SPREAD	FLOWERS AND FOLIAGE	NOTES
Clematis 'Jackmanii Superba'	3 × 1m/10 × 3ft	Deep purple flowers in midsummer	Shade roots but grow rest of plant in sun
Geranium wallichianum 'Buxton's Variety'	50 × 60cm/20 × 24in	Almost blue flowers with pale eye in late summer to autumn	Latest flowering hardy geranium; grow in sun or light shade
Lavandula angustifolia 'Hidcote'	0.6 × 1m/2 × 3ft	Spikes of purple with silvery foliage	Dislikes damp or shade
Monarda 'Capricorn'	70 × 40cm/28 × 16in	Deep violet flowers in late summer	Dislikes drought and poor or clay soils
Perovskia atriplicifolia	1 × 0.5m/3ft × 1ft 8in	Richly aromatic foliage and lovely blue-mauve flowers in late summer	Needs sun and good drainage
Salvia × *sylvestris* 'Mainacht'	40 × 60cm/16 × 24in	Deep blue-purple flowers in midsummer	Grow in sun; good for dry soils

all colour schemes. This is hardly surprising given that the range of possible plants in these colours is vast. Combining them is easy, and there are the additional advantages that they are almost unfailingly hardy and reliable and have low maintenance requirements. Soft colours like this more often are a great success in climates where the skies are often grey and overcast, but they are less successful in areas where the light is strong and soft tones are not as easily appreciated.

Pastel shades make us feel soothed and relaxed, which is a major reason for their popularity. They are virtually foolproof to combine, and the skill involved in making a pastel border has more to do

RIGHT: Foxgloves, opium poppies and polemonium are easy pastel companions in early summer. All self-seed readily.

OPPOSITE: A startling spring combination: yellow *Euphorbia polychroma* with tulips and wallflowers.

Best soft pinks

	HEIGHT × SPREAD	FLOWERS AND FOLIAGE	NOTES
Astilbe 'Venus'	1 × 1m/3 × 3ft	Plumes of flower in early summer	Needs moist soil
Geranium × *oxonianum* 'Wargrave Pink'	40 × 50cm/16 × 20in	Salmon pink flowers throughout summer	Tolerant
Malva moschata	50 × 30cm/20 × 12in	Large pale pink flowers in early summer	Needs sun; short lived
Penstemon 'Apple Blossom'	60 × 70cm/24 × 28in	Bushy perennial with tubular flowers in spikes in late summer	Short lived; dislikes cold
Rosa 'Constance Spry'	2 × 1.5m/6 × 5ft	Rounded double flowers with a spicy scent all summer long	Can be trained as a climber
Rosa 'The Fairy'	60 × 60cm/2 × 2ft	Mass of pale pink flowers on a compact bush in late summer and autumn	

ABOVE: Complementary colours, like these yellow bearded irises and blue nigella, are a powerful combination.
RIGHT: Vivid colour groups work best if plenty of 'buffer colours', such as yellow-green
nicotiana and alchemilla, are included.

with ensuring a long season of interest than it has to do with colour combination. Pink- and white-flowering shrubs like *Viburnum* species are a good way to start the year, perhaps with pale yellow daffodils and the softer shades of tulip. The main season is early summer, when old-fashioned roses are at their best, underplanted with hardy *Geranium* species. Other perennials, notably asters, can be used to continue the season. Pink gets notably less frequent as summer progresses, but the blues, lavenders and purples of asters become more important. Pink annuals and half-hardy plants, like pelargoniums, can be used to fill this gap, however.

Pastel shades, pink especially, consort well with silver foliage, which helps to add a bit of sparkle – lavenders, artemesias and silver grasses are possibilities – but if you feel that too many pastel colours are a bit safe and you want to add some extra brilliance, try adding some darker colours. Strong magenta flowers, for instance, look a lot less violent when they

are mixed with paler pinks and silver foliage, and they are quietened down most effectively by being paired with pale blue flowers or the yellow-green of euphorbias. The strange, pale yellow-green flowers of euphorbias give an interesting lift to pastel borders, and the long flowering season, often starting quite early in the year, is particularly appreciated. Other pale yellows can be included too, but many people feel that darker yellows do not combine well with pink.

Recent years have seen the introduction of dark shades, almost black, of common annuals, like sweet peas and cornflowers. These, especially when they are placed next to silver foliage, are one of the best ways to add spice to pastel compositions, and they always provoke interest.

Contrasting Colours

Pastel shades, one-colour borders, white gardens — if all these recently fashionable ideas seem too safe and middle-of-the-road for you, you are in good company. A lot of people like to plant vibrant bedding displays, continuing the tradition established by the Victorian colour theorists who claimed that contrast was best.

Composing a mixed border with contrasting colours does require more skill and care than working with a combination of annuals and bedding plants however — unsuccessful combinations are not so easily pulled up at the end of the year. The best thing to do is to work with a particular combination that you feel happy with — violet-purple and yellow, for example — and make it dominant in the border, choosing theme and secondary plants accordingly. Other contrasting colours, perhaps a few reds and whites, can be added to play a supporting role.

White, cream and yellow-green flowers have a special role to play in borders of contrasting colours. Including some of these as secondary plants or filler plants is one way of ensuring that your colour scheme will please a good number of people. They are 'buffer colours', especially when they are planted to separate strong vibrant colours. In these circumstances they provide a cool contrast and allow the other colours to be appreciated for their own sakes rather than as foils to other strong colours.

Best silver-grey foliage

	HEIGHT × SPREAD	FLOWERS AND FOLIAGE	NOTES
Artemesia ludoviciana	0.5 × 1m/1ft 8in × 3ft	Silver-white leaves	Gets untidy later in the season
Ballota pseudodictamnus	0.6 × 1.2m/2 × 4ft	Grey-green, rather woolly foliage	Looks at its best in late winter; not for cold areas or damp spots
Elymus magellanicus	40 × 50cm/16 × 20in	The bluest leaved plant there is; neat, non-spreading tufts of more or less evergreen grassy leaves	Ideal for dotting around the border between perennials
Lamium maculatum 'Beacon Silver'	0.2 × 1m/8in × 3ft	Silver evergreen leaves; pink flowers in spring	Unlike other silver plants, it thrives in shade

8

Mixed Border Plants

SHRUBS AND PERENNIALS are the two plant forms that feature in the mixed border, but many gardeners include bulbs, climbers, annuals and even the odd tree. This chapter looks at each of these plant forms and considers their place and potential in the mixed border.

The diagrams that accompany each section show at a glance the role played by the particular plant form – shrubs, perennials, trees and so on – in the border in spring and summer. The coloured outline represents the plant form under discussion.

SHRUBS

Shrubs are woody, like trees, but they tend to be smaller and have multiple stems emerging at ground level. It is primarily the mixture of shrubs with perennials that makes the mixed border 'mixed', and for many gardeners, shrubs are the backbone of the

Shrubs

Spring

Summer

border, providing permanence and structure, especially when all other life has retreated underground in winter. Some shrubs, and indeed some trees, add structure to the border because they are kept clipped, as geometric shapes or topiary, but shrubs, or at least large shrubs, are not essential to the mixed border.

While the sense of structure that shrubs give is a fundamental reason for growing them in the border,

Vivid colours seem to work well in autumn. The leaves of a *Cornus* (dogwood) provide a backdrop to an aster.

it is the flowers of most that are the reason for their popularity, especially since most flower in the first half of the year before other plants begin to bloom. In addition, many have attractive berries at the end of the year.

Shrubs have become the mainstay of many a border because of their low maintenance needs. The odd one may flower better if it is pruned skilfully, but on the whole, once they are established, they will give years of pleasure without the gardener needing to lift a finger.

It has to be said, however, that shrubs usually lack an interesting habit of growth, and they can look dull after flowering, which means that in the second half of the year they are little more than a green mass. Many grow into quite large plants, too large for the small garden, and the gardener who happily bought half a dozen from the garden centre four years ago may begin to regret the purchase.

Of all shrubs roses are the most popular. Yet they are all too often disease-ridden and involve the gardener in a lot of extra work. In fact, many roses are untidy by nature, and they do suffer from a variety of diseases, especially when they are under stress. They flourish on deep, fertile soils and positively love heavy clays, but they do not tend to do well on thin or sandy soils. Perhaps people should be more selective about growing them. If they do flourish,

they make good theme plants for the border, especially if long- or recurrent-flowering varieties are chosen. The old-fashioned or shrub kinds, with soft pink flowers, consort well with many perennials.

Shrubs, then, need to be chosen carefully. Many mixed borders will need only two or three if they are not to be swallowed up in years to come, and the qualities to look for are early flowering and scent.

DWARF SHRUBS

Low-growing woody plants like heathers and lavenders are technically shrubs. Their small size makes them useful in the mixed border, not just to put at the front (their usual place) but also to be dotted around, as they too will provide year-round structure, like their larger cousins. The great advantage of nearly all of them is that they are evergreen, often

Flowering shrubs

	HEIGHT × SPREAD	FLOWERS AND FOLIAGE	NOTES
Berberis darwinii	2 × 2m/6 × 6ft	Neat evergreen foliage; yellow flowers in spring; dark blue berries in autumn	Dislikes extremely dry and cold areas
Buddleia davidii	4 × 4m/13 × 13ft	Mauve spikes attract vast numbers of butterflies in summer	Tolerant of a wide range of conditions; 'Nanho' varieties are smaller
Ceanothus × veitchianus	3 × 3m/10 × 10ft	Deep blue flowers smother neat evergreen leaves in early summer	Does best on poor, dry soils; dislikes cold or exposure
Chaenomeles 'Crimson and Gold'	3 × 3m/10 × 10ft	Scarlet flowers over a long winter–spring season	Tolerates wide range of conditions
Hebe 'Midsummer Beauty'	1.2 × 1.2m/4 × 4ft	Blue-mauve spikes turn almost white as they age; flowers over long period in summer; evergreen foliage	Good for windy and mild maritime areas; dislikes cold
Rhododendron yakushimanum	1 × 1.5m/3 × 5ft	Neat hemisphere of dark evergreen leaves; pale pink flowers in late spring	Dislikes lime and drought

Good purple-leaved shrubs are rare – *Cotinus coggygria* 'Royal Purple' is one of the best.

Dwarf shrubs

Spring

Summer

Foliage shrubs

	HEIGHT × SPREAD	FLOWERS AND FOLIAGE	NOTES
Cotinus coggygria 'Royal Purple'	4 × 4m/13 × 13ft	The deepest purple foliage of any shrub	'Smoke-like' seedheads in autumn
Elaeagnus pungens 'Maculata'	2 × 2m/6 × 6ft	Constantly cheerful golden-variegated evergreen foliage	Look out for reverting green shoots; dislikes intense cold
Ilex × altaclerensis 'Golden King'	4 × 2m/13 × 6ft	Fine golden-variegated evergreen foliage; red berries	Compact habit
Laurus nobilis	4 × 4m/13 × 13ft	Dark green evergreen leaves	Compact habit; easily kept small or shaped by clipping; dislikes cold or windy areas
Mahonia 'Charity'	3 × 2m/10 × 6ft	Holly-like evergreen leaves; scented yellow flowers in winter	Upright habit
Pieris japonica	2 × 3m/6 × 10ft	Fiery red young growth in spring, maturing to dark, glossy evergreen leaves	Slow growing; dislikes lime, drought or severe frost

ABOVE: Roses are good while they are in flower,
but remember that they are dull in leaf!
LEFT: Shrubs with contrasting leaf colour
are effective for a long season.

quite attractively so, as can be seen, for example, in the silvery leaved lavenders and golden heathers. Nearly all are tidy growers when they are young, although annual pruning is often necessary as they get older. The close hummocky or ground-hugging habit of many dwarf shrubs means that they are easier to keep in tidy shape than larger ones.

Perhaps the greatest advantage of the main groups of dwarf shrubs is that they are naturally plants of harsh environments and are thus ideal for the kind of garden that at first can induce despair: windy, coastal or bone dry locations. Heathers,

dwarf rhododendrons and many similar plants can be used in windy locations where the soil is acidic, infertile and quite hostile to most garden plants. The 'heather garden' is outside the scope of this book, but any gardener trying to make a border on such a site would be well advised to incorporate a wide range of these versatile plants. Similarly, the gardener in areas where summer drought is a feature of the climate could use silvery Mediterranean dwarf shrubs like lavenders, cistus and santolina as the backbone of the border.

HERBACEOUS PERENNIALS

The terminology of this group is a bit complicated and causes great confusion, so let's get it right. 'Perennial' simply means that a plant lives for several years and does not die after flowering and seeding (in fact, trees and shrubs are, strictly speaking,

border, although they are being grown in a more relaxed and informal way than previously. For the gardener with a small or medium sized garden, with only limited border space, it is essential that perennials are seen as the dominant group for the border. Their relatively small size means that far more perennials than shrubs can be fitted into a confined space, with all this implies for seasonal interest and opportunities to create an interesting composition.

Perennial flowers display an enormously wide range of colour and form, and many also have attractive foliage. The sheer range of shapes, sizes and possibilities they present is staggering. The main perennial season starts in early summer and reaches

———————————— ✦ ————————————

RIGHT: Later in the season, perennial colours –
an orange hemerocallis and a purple penstemon – are
still strong.

Perennials, such as penstemon, heuchera and
artemisia, are the mainstay of the summer border.

———————————— ✦ ————————————

perennials). 'Herbaceous' means that the plant is non-woody and dies down in winter, to re-emerge the following spring. As far as most gardeners are concerned, however, 'perennial' means 'herbaceous perennial'. Just to complicate matters, some herbaceous perennials are effectively evergreen – hellebores and periwinkles (*Vinca* species), for example.

The traditional herbaceous border was the place where perennials were displayed, but with the rise of a more low-maintenance style of gardening, perennials went out of fashion and were displaced by shrubs. Now things have changed and perennials are being given back their rightful place in the

Herbaceous perennials

Spring

Summer

a crescendo in late summer, with a good many options for autumn. The only reason that many gardeners complain that 'late summer is a dull time in the garden' is that the spectacular later flowering perennials were out of fashion for some time and are still not always freely available.

Perennials, dying back as they do every winter, have to grow fast to reach their full size in summer. Not surprisingly, the larger ones do best on fertile soils with plentiful moisture, while many smaller perennials are more tolerant of poorer soils. Nevertheless, the remarkable thing about the majority of perennials is their adaptability to a wide range of conditions.

Perhaps the supreme advantage of perennials as border plants is the speed with which they establish themselves — many three-year-old plants look as if they have been there for far longer. Shrubs, on the other hand, take many more years to show their full potential. In addition, many perennials are easy to propagate by simply dividing the plants in spring — splitting one large plant into many smaller ones — which makes ambitious border schemes relatively inexpensive to realize.

The disadvantage of perennials is that there are few spring-flowering ones (but then there are plenty of bulbs instead), and the fact that they inevitably require some maintenance. The annual growth cycle of a perennial involves the production of stems and leaves that die back in autumn, necessitating an annual clearing at the very least.

Early perennials

	HEIGHT × SPREAD	FLOWERS AND FOLIAGE	NOTES
Bergenia varieties	30 × 50cm/12 × 20in	Magenta, pink or white flowers, often early, above glossy evergreen leaves, which may turn red in winter	Tolerant
Euphorbia polychroma	30 × 60cm/1 × 2ft	Green-yellow flowers in spring combine well with bright bulbs	Dislikes drought
Helleborus orientalis hybrids	50 × 60cm/20 × 24in	Cream, white or purple flowers, often spotted or streaked, in winter to spring; distinctive glossy evergreen foliage	Sun or light shade
Lamium maculatum varieties	20 × 50cm/8 × 20in	Pink or white flowers above silver- or white-streaked foliage in spring; more or less evergreen	Good ground cover; tolerant of sun or shade
Pulmonaria varieties	30 × 50cm/12 × 20in	Blue, mauve or pinkish-red flowers over a long late winter to spring season; many varieties with evergreen, silver-splashed foliage	Good in shade

Late perennials

	HEIGHT × SPREAD	FLOWERS AND FOLIAGE	NOTES
Anemone × hybrida 'Honorine Jobert'	1.2 × 0.6m/4 × 2ft	Large, pure white flowers	Long-lived plants; good in light shade
Aster cordifolius 'Little Carlow'	80 × 40cm/32 × 16in	Mauve-blue daisy flowers	
Aster × frikartii 'Mönch'	70 × 40cm/28 × 16in	Blue daisy flowers over a long midsummer to autumn season	
Leucanthemella serotina	1.2 × 0.5m/4ft × 1ft 8in	Large, pure white daisies on upright stems at end of season	Can spread in moist soil
Rudbeckia fulgida var. *sullivantii* 'Goldsturm'	50 × 60cm/20 × 24in	Yellow daisies with dark centres in late summer to early autumn	Compact habit
Schizostylis coccinea	60 × 30cm/2 × 1ft	Red or pink, depending on variety, flowers above grassy foliage	Does best in mild areas where it can flower for most of winter

Best overall perennials

	HEIGHT × SPREAD	FLOWERS AND FOLIAGE	NOTES
Alchemilla mollis	0.4 × 1m/16 × 39in	Green flowers	Fine scalloped leaves; a good backdrop for other plants; sun or shade; seedlings can be invasive
Geranium endressii; *G. × oxonianum* varieties	30–50 × 40–70cm/ 12–20 × 16–28in	Pink flowers in early summer; more flushes later	Showy low ground-cover habit makes these good filler plants; sun or shade
Hemerocallis 'Golden Chimes'	60 × 60cm/24 × 24in	Delicate, yellow, trumpet-shaped flowers; grassy foliage in early to midsummer	Reliable
Iris sibirica varieties	80 × 40cm/32 × 16in	Blue or violet flowers in early summer	Short season but reliable, tolerant and long lived
Sedum spectabile	40 × 60cm/16 × 24in	Dull pinkish-red flowers from late summer are a magnet for butterflies	Interesting fleshy foliage; needs sun
Stachys olympica	30 × 80cm/12 × 32in	Woolly silver leaves	Good front of border or filler plant; excellent backdrop for colour

ORNAMENTAL GRASSES

The use of ornamental grasses is a newish trend in gardening. For our purposes 'grasses' include plants like sedges and wood rushes, which are actually botanically distinct. Most are grown for the texture of their flower- and seedheads or for the combination of this with their foliage. Their colours are soft – mostly browns, yellows and fawns – which makes them easy to blend with practically anything else. This neutral colouring comes into its own when it is used as 'buffer' for strong flower colours. The textures and forms, usually soft and yielding, but sometimes bold, offer a contrast to more conventional flowering perennials and shrubs.

Some grasses are grown for their foliage, the evergreen clumps of many species providing useful ground cover for shady or difficult parts of the border, or the strong blues, yellows or reds of others making an attractive source of long-season colour.

The best season for grasses is late summer and autumn, which is when the majority of species produce their decorative seedheads. Most will continue to look good until well into winter, and many look fabulous when covered with hoar frost. In fact, they are probably the most rewarding category of plant for this difficult early-winter period, when even the snowdrops seem a distant dream.

It is widely believed that grasses make invasive border plants, but this is simply not true. A few do spread invasively, but the greater proportion of them are no worse or better than the rapidly spreading perennials or shrubs that can get out of hand.

Ornamental grasses and grass-like plants

	HEIGHT × SPREAD	FLOWERS AND FOLIAGE	NOTES
Calamagrostis × acutiflora 'Karl Foerster'	1.2 × 0.4m/4ft × 1ft 4in	Strongly upright, pale brown heads	Superb vertical emphasis among lower planting for late summer
Carex pendula	0.7 × 1m/28 × 39in	Catkin-like heads on arching stems in summer; evergreen dark green leaves	Elegant but can self-seed invasively; good in shade, including dry shade
Milium effusum 'Aureum'	40 × 30cm/16 × 12in	Yellowish-green leaves and flowerheads	Lovely with yellow or purple flowers or foliage in early summer; best in light shade
Miscanthus sinensis varieties	1–2.5 × 1.5m/3–8 × 5ft	Silvery or pink heads in late summer; continue looking good until winter	Spectacular and useful ornamental grass; varieties cover a wide range of heights
Stipa arundinacea	60 × 50cm/24 × 20in	Tuft-forming, olive green grass that becomes orangey in winter	Dislikes extreme cold
Stipa gigantea	2 × 2.1m/6 × 7ft		Oat-like heads on long, graceful stems from early summer to early winter

The perennial grass pennisetum and half-hardy and bedding plants are a novel combination for a sunny spot in late summer.

Ornamental grasses

Spring

Summer

BULBS

Bulbs are essentially perennials that come in an easily packaged form. The beauty of bulbs is that they are so easy to obtain and to plant and they give gratifying and almost instantaneous results. The vast majority are spring flowering, which makes them the mainstay of the border in the earlier part of the year. Their colour range is remarkably wide, with especially good blues and yellows.

The annual growth cycle of bulbs is designed to get their flowering, growing and seeding out of the way before shrubs, perennials and grasses take over. They are thus tailor-made to fit in around other

Bulbs, such as tulips and narcissi, make spring
gardening remarkably easy and rewarding.

———— ❖ ————

There are also a number of summer-flowering and,
more importantly, autumn-flowering ones. The
latter include hardy cyclamen and the various plants
that go under the name 'autumn crocus'.

As border plants, bulbs have few drawbacks, but
they are worth mentioning. All bulbs depend on
having their leaves unmolested for as long as they
last so that they are able to lay down reserves of
nutrients for the following year's flowers. Consequently, those leaves must not be cut or 'tidied up'
after the flowers have finished, and they can look
messy – daffodils are notoriously so. Some bulbs,
tulips especially, often do not flower well after their
first year; these bulbs originate from climates where
they get baked by the hot sun for several months
after flowering, and they will not flower again if they
do not get this. Since this does not happen in many
borders, these bulbs should be replaced every year.

Bulbs

Spring

Summer

plants, filling the gaps in the border while the
bulkier plants get moving in spring. Many are also
suitable for growing under deciduous trees, where
they take advantage of the leafless conditions to
make the most of the available light.

It is not only in spring that bulbs flower, of course.

Spring bulbs

	HEIGHT × SPREAD	FLOWERS AND FOLIAGE	NOTES
Crocus vernus	10 × 6cm/4 × 2½in	Pale mauve flowers in late winter	Naturalizes well; sun or light shade
Fritillaria meleagris	30 × 5cm/12 × 2in	Strange but attractive nodding, chequered-purple flowers in late spring	One of the few bulbs suitable for damp soils
Muscari aucheri	10 × 5cm/4 × 2in	Deep blue spikes in mid-spring	Naturalizes well in sunny places
Narcissus 'Actaea'	40 × 10cm/16 × 4in	Fragrant white flowers with a shallow orange central cup	Naturalizes well in sun or light shade
Narcissus 'February Gold'	30 × 10cm/12 × 4in	Yellow trumpets in early spring	Naturalizes well in sun or light shade
Tulipa kaufmanniana varieties	10–30 × 15cm/4–12 × 6in	Red, pink, orange, cream or yellow flowers in early to mid-spring	Attractively marked leaves; needs full sun

Summer bulbs

	HEIGHT × SPREAD	FLOWERS AND FOLIAGE	NOTES
Allium giganteum	1.8 × 0.3m/6 × 1ft	Mauve, spherical flowerheads on thin stems	A dramatic spectacle, especially viewed above low-growing plants; needs full sun
Camassia quamash	60 × 30cm/24 × 12in	Blue flowers in spikes	Forms clumps in time; likes moist soils
Canna 'Wyoming'	80 × 40cm/32 × 16in	Dark purple-stained leaves and red flowers make a dramatic sight	Many other varieties; needs sun and a fertile, preferably moist soil; half hardy
Crocosmia 'Emily McKenzie'	60 × 20cm/24 × 8in	Dramatic orange flowers with central blotch; sword-shaped leaves	Not hardy in cold areas
Fritillaria imperialis	1.5 × 0.3m/5 × 1ft	Orange or yellow flowers in a statuesque stem	Needs full sun
Lilium regale	1 × 0.2m/39 × 8in	Fantastically fragrant white trumpets	Needs full sun

CLIMBERS

There was once a time when a book on making a border would devote little space to climbing plants. Nowadays people are being much more imaginative at planting with climbers, so enabling them to play a greater part in the border.

We can define a climber as being a plant that cannot support itself, so leans on and climbs up something else, usually a tree or shrub, so that it can reach up into the light. There is an indistinct halfway category, that of 'lax shrubs', which are weak stemmed and tend to fall over without some support – many large roses fall (quite literally) into this category. They look untidy in the border unless they are given some support, such as a framework around them, or are trained against a wall.

A border backed by a wall or fence provides the obvious place for climbing plants, because they can become part of the backdrop for the free-standing plants of the border. Few climbers climb unaided, most needing the support of wire or trellis to cling to. Supports can be made that enable climbers to be used as free-standing plants in the border. They can be utilitarian or can be made into decorative items in their own right, such as obelisks and arches (see page 91). Climbing roses are frequently included in borders, either on backdrops or on free-standing supports like arches. Some can get enormous, filling

Climbers

	HEIGHT × SPREAD	FLOWERS AND FOLIAGE	NOTES
Clematis armandii	6m/20ft	White flowers in spring among exotic-looking glossy evergreen foliage	Dislikes cold or exposed situations
Clematis montana	10m/33ft	White or pink flowers in late spring	Strong-growing plant; good for covering high walls; tolerates wide range of conditions
Clematis viticella	3m/10ft	Varieties available in red, pink, white or purple	Perfect for mid- or late summer colour on smaller fences or free-standing supports; dislikes drought
Hedera helix 'Gold Heart'	4m/13ft	Golden-variegated evergreen leaves	Self-clinging plant; suitable for shade or full sun
Lonicera periclymenum 'Graham Thomas'	3m/10ft	Richly scented pale yellow flowers from midsummer to autumn	Dislikes thin or dry soils
Parthenocissus quinquefolia (Virginia creeper)	4m/13ft	Glossy leaves; spectacular orange autumn colour	Self-clinging foliage plant; good for covering walls and fences or for rambling through trees or large shrubs

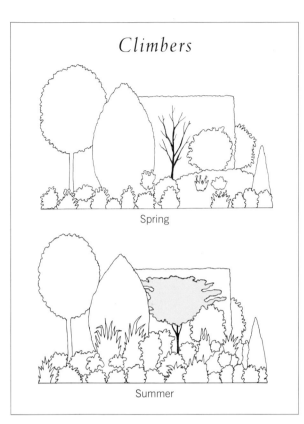

Climbers

Spring

Summer

Like many climbers, *Clematis viticella* 'Madame Julia Correvon' needs a cool base but a sunny top.

entire trees, so varieties must be chosen carefully, especially if they are to be grown on a support.

Climbers in the border are perhaps not the ideal subject for the gardener who is anxious to save on labour or who is perhaps inexperienced in dealing with plants. One on a wall or fence will need little care after the initial training on to some supports, but a climber grown on a free-standing support or over a shrub needs to be carefully selected, particularly for size, and will require sensitive pruning and training if it is to look at its best.

ANNUALS

Annuals are plants that live for one year only, producing plentiful seed after flowering and then dying. As far as the gardener is concerned the category also includes a variety of plants that are in fact perennial but that are grown as annuals, of which the bright

red bedding salvia is a good example and bedding pelargoniums (usually called geraniums) another. So called 'half-hardy annuals' are started off from seed in spring under glass, planted out in early summer and then die after the first frosts. Hardy annuals are those that can be sown into the ground in the place where they are to flower from early spring on.

Annuals have two great advantages in borders: they are colourful and reliably so, looking their best in late summer, and they are quick to establish, reaching their peak only a few months after planting. They are thus ideal for temporary gap filling.

There are two traditions of annual planting. One

is the cottage garden approach, which relied on hardy annuals and resulted in the informal mixing of predominantly pastel-shaded flowers with perennials and other plants. The other approach is the highly formal public park-type display, which is based on the use of highly coloured, mostly half-hardy, annuals, usually in rigid patterns. The latter tradition has little to offer the creator of a mixed border, yet some of the plants it uses can profitably be combined with perennials and other border plants, if strong late-summer colour is wanted.

The world of annuals is changing fast, as many new varieties are being introduced for the first time in many years. The majority are softer in shade than the old-style half-hardy varieties and have a more informal habit of growth – they are, in fact, more

Annual cosmos mixes colourfully with *Verbena bonariensis*, an annual in colder climates.

Annuals

Spring

Summer

Hardy annuals			
	HEIGHT × SPREAD	FLOWERS AND FOLIAGE	NOTES
Borago officinalis	60 × 30cm/24 × 12in	Pure blue flowers and hairy leaves	
Brachycome iberidifolia	40 × 40cm/16 × 16in	Blue daisies and a long flowering period	
Calendula officinalis varieties	40 × 50cm/16 × 20in	Yellow and orange flowers over a long season	
Limnanthes douglasii	15 × 10cm/6 × 4in	White-edged yellow flowers for most of summer	
Nigella damascena 'Persian Jewels'	50 × 20m/20 × 8in	Blue, pink and white flowers among feathery foliage	Often self-seeds
Papaver somniferum varieties	70 × 30cm/28 × 12in	Pink, purple and white flowers; grey leaves	Usually self-seeds

like the cottage garden hardy annuals. The possibilities that lie in combining late-summer perennials with annuals are more exciting than ever before.

The main disadvantage with using annuals in borders is the amount of labour involved, which includes preparing the ground, sowing and planting, sometimes watering and then clearing away at the end of the year.

TREES

Trees in a border? Well, more probably one tree! Many gardeners will already have a tree in their garden and may have to include it in their mixed border whether they want to or not. So, they are virtually forced to have a shady border, at least in part. But what about planting a tree?

There are plenty of small trees that will cast only a small area of shade as they grow and that are thus entirely suitable for inclusion in borders, at least in ones that are not too restricted in size. Small trees make fine centrepieces to island beds, where the border is completely surrounded by lawn or paving, but there is no reason why they cannot be put in borders with a backdrop.

The advantages of using trees in borders is that they add scale, both to the border and the garden, and can help to link the garden to the wider landscape. Many trees have attractive shapes and branching patterns, which are particularly noticeable if they drop their leaves in winter. Flowering varieties often bloom in spring, when there is little other colour, and far more trees than any other category of plant form have good autumn colour.

What should you look for when selecting a tree for a border? Above all, it must be small so that its eventual size will not completely overshadow the border. Select a tree with a good shape because you will find yourself choosing quite enough shapeless shrubs and untidy perennials as it is. Many small trees sold for small gardens have an attractive upright habit, which will minimize the amount of shade cast and provide at least one large, neat shape.

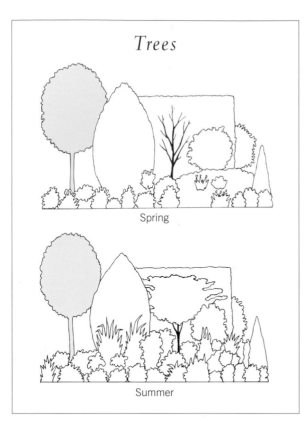

Trees

Spring

Summer

Evergreens, conifers especially, cast year-round shade that makes it difficult to grow anything underneath them. Any conifer that is chosen should be narrow, like a cypress.

Some deciduous trees, such as many maples (*Acer* species), are so efficient at drawing moisture and nutrients out of the soil that they make life difficult for smaller plants around them. Birches and most species grown for their flowers, such as cherries (*Prunus* species), apples (*Malus* species) and rowans (*Sorbus* species), are not so greedy, so they co-exist with other plants more easily.

Some trees can be effectively miniaturized by grafting on to slow-growing rootstocks – notably apples (both eating and ornamental) on M27 rootstocks – which will allow you to have some of the

RIGHT: Apricot foxgloves subtly pick up the colour of the purple-leaved elder behind.

Small trees

	HEIGHT × SPREAD	FLOWERS AND FOLIAGE	NOTES
Acer palmatum	5 × 5m/16 × 16ft	Excellent foliage with spectacular autumn colour	Wide range of varieties, including dwarf forms; dislikes wind and drought
Amelanchier canadensis	7 × 5m/23 × 16ft	White flowers in spring; purple fruit in autumn; brilliant orange autumn colour	Dislikes drought
Betula jacquemontii	12 × 5m/29 × 16ft	Glistening white bark, so a good winter tree	Casts light shade; hardy and tolerant
Malus tschonoskii	11 × 4m/36 × 13ft	Pale pink flowers in spring; bright orange autumn colour	Upright shape; casts little shade
Prunus 'Pandora'	10 × 7m/33 × 23ft	Pale pink flowers; orange-yellow foliage in autumn	More or less upright shape
Sorbus commixta 'Jermyns'	12 × 8m/39 × 26ft	White flowers in spring; red fruits in autumn	Attractive foliage

advantages of a tree but without any problems of size. Also enjoying some popularity are 'top-grafted shrubs', which are shrubs or small trees grafted on to a straight stem, much like the (now rather out of fashion) standard roses. It should be borne in mind that the stem will not grow beyond the 1.5–2 metres/5–6 feet it is in the garden centre and the top may well form an untidy mop after a few years. In my opinion, such creations completely lack the proportion and elegance of true trees.

SEASONAL PLANTINGS

Formal Victorian bedding schemes usually incorporated a few centrepiece foliage plants such palms, bananas or agaves. This idea is being revived by the use of various tender plants in garden borders. Plants normally grown in conservatories are either put outside for summer in containers or actually

A columnar yew transforms this otherwise shapeless planting as it reaches for the skies.

Seasonal planting

Spring

Summer

planted out for the warmer months. They add an exotic touch to a border, which is particularly valuable where dramatic foliage is needed, because there are some subtropical foliage shapes that are never found among hardy plants. Such shapes make an excellent focal point for a border. Many conservatory plants, especially flowering ones, are prone to infestation with pests, and putting them outside for summer is the best way of keeping them healthy. Even house plants can be put outside in summer if they are in a sheltered border; the results certainly surprise and amuse.

Recent years have seen the growing popularity of so-called 'patio plants' – marguerites (*Argyranthemum* species), for instance – which are planted out for summer and then dug up again and taken indoors for winter, or cuttings are taken and protected until planting out next spring. These free-flowering and colourful plants have joined the ranks of more established species like dahlias, cannas and gladioli, the roots of which are lifted every autumn and overwintered inside. Particularly valued pelargoniums are often treated in this way, rather than letting them die with the frost as happens with the cheaper bedding varieties.

While such imaginative bedding out does add an extra dimension to a border, it is quite exacting. Planting out and digging up again in autumn is labour intensive and has to be done on time, otherwise early frosts may easily kill or damage valued plants. Many patio plants do not die down to convenient tubers like dahlias and require cultivation in frost-free and well-lit conditions over winter.

Fruit and vegetables

Spring

Summer

Ideas for good-looking fruit, vegetables and herbs

Tree fruit
Chiefly apples, pears, plums and cherries; have attractive soft pink or white spring flowers

Herbs
- Chives: pinkish-mauve flowers in summer
- Fennel: feather foliage
- Lovage: erect growth; attractive foliage
- Rosemary: dark evergreen foliage; blue flowers in summer
- Sage: Purple-grey evergreen foliage

Vegetables
- Asparagus: plumes of feathery foliage
- Globe artichoke: architectural, large thistle-like stems and flowers
- Leaf beet 'Ruby Chard': glowing red stems
- Lettuce, Lolla Rossa, 'Red Salad Bowl': varieties with red-hued leaves
- Runner bean: scarlet flowers

FRUIT, VEGETABLES AND HERBS

Edible and culinary plants were customarily given their own section of the garden, often hidden behind a screen of hedging, as if there were something inherently shameful about a row of broad beans or a clump of parsley. Increasingly though, adventurous gardeners are using fruit, vegetables and herbs in borders and integrating them with purely ornamental plants. If only a few vegetables or fruit bushes are needed, this is perfectly practical way of growing them.

Fruit trees such as apples and cherries are attractive in their own right, notably when they are in flower, which makes them worthwhile additions to the border, although care must be taken to prevent other plants, vigorous perennials especially, from growing too close to the roots, which could reduce their growth and cropping. Soft fruit is not always

Why not combine fruit with flowers? Established fruit trees will tolerate some perennials and annuals around their bases, although younger trees will not.

so obviously a part of the border – raspberry canes have little aesthetic appeal! Blackberries and other climbing soft fruit can, however, be quite attractive if they are trained on a fence or wall as part of a border, and some gooseberry and currant varieties have fruit that is ornamental.

While some vegetables do undeniably look unattractive (Brussels sprouts are a prime example), many have ornamental qualities, including runner bean flowers, pumpkins and squashes in fruit, red beetroot, oakleaf lettuce and, especially, the stunning crimson of ruby chard. Mindful of this newfound artistic strand of gardening, some seed producers have brought out varieties that are grown as much for their decorative qualities as for their culinary ones, particularly among lettuces and beetroot.

Realistically, most gardeners will devote only a small part of their borders to fruit and vegetables. Vegetables come and go quickly, and so tend to leave gaps. Herbs, however, are nearly all soundly perennial and are harvested only a little at a time, making them much better as permanent border plants. Some, such as sage (*Salvia officinalis*) and rosemary (*Rosmarinus officinalis*), are grown as ornamentals at least as often as they are grown as herbs. Others, such as lovage (*Levisticum officinalis*) and chives (*Allium schoenoprasum*), may not be in the front line of ornamental plants, but they are tidy and attractive enough to be included in a mixed border.

9

Practical Points

*L*AYING OUT A NEW BORDER starts with preparing the site, which may well be done several months before planting, the summer preceding autumn planting being the traditional and best time. The final selection of plants needs to be made, a plan drawn up and the plants ordered. Finally, the plants are laid out and planted.

PREPARING THE SITE

The traditional border was always intensively prepared, often with the incorporation of large quantities of manure or other composted material to improve the soil. Soils that were heavy, or light, or in some other way deviated from the ideal were seen as 'problem' soils and thus in need of even more preparatory work.

A modern mixed border allows a more flexible approach to be taken. As we saw on pages 35–8, if plants are chosen that will grow naturally well on the soil in your garden, 'soil improvement' comes to be seen less as a vital piece of preparation and more as an unnecessary expense, costly to both wallet and back. Nevertheless, if you do have a soil that restricts the range of plants that you want to grow, it is natural that you will want to do some work on making it more acceptable to a wider range of plants. This can be done selectively, by working on small areas or a frontal strip, for example, so that some annuals and bedding can be grown on improved soil among woody plants and perennials that have been chosen as more suitable for the prevailing conditions.

'Difficult' soils tend to fall into one of three categories: clay/heavy, which is often badly drained but fertile; sandy/light/stony, which is usually poor and often dry; and chalk/limestone/alkaline, which is often thin and therefore poor and dry. If you are happy to rely entirely on those shrubs, climbers, bulbs and perennials that are content to grow on the existing soil, little preparatory work will need be done beyond removing weeds. You can go straight on to planting (see pages 142–4).

Trying to grow a wider range of plants, especially those showier annuals, bedding plants and perennials that are the feature of the classic late-summer border, will necessitate some extra input if the soil falls short of the ideal easily worked loam. The most effective input is organic matter – home-made compost, commercial compost, well-rotted manure, waste agricultural products, such as mushroom compost and so on. Such material breaks down to form humus, which holds water and nutrients in the soil (which is useful on sandy and thin soils) and which makes clay soils less sticky. Heavy or light soils will, however, need many years' generous application of such material before an appreciable difference is felt. Various soil conditioners are also available for the improvement of problem soils, especially heavy ones. It is only worthwhile looking into these if your garden soil is badly drained or is going to be worked annually for growing bedding plants, for instance.

Traditional garden practice (which always seems to involve as much hard work as possible) is to dig in such organic matter and soil conditioners deeply, to the depth of two spade blades. Working a soil to this depth, which has the effect of breaking down any hard layers in the soil that might discourage penetration by roots, does undoubtedly work wonders, but given that it is such hard work, its necessity must be questioned. I would say that it is vital only for vegetables and for the very best displays of perennials and annuals. It is easier to dig organic matter into the top layer of the soil (the depth of one spade blade) and to rely on the worms to carry it down further.

Bulbs that always come back

Some bulbs, such as many tulips, need hot sun for several months to 'ripen' the bulbs for flowering again the following year. The following bulbs will reliably flower year after year and increase in number if planted in the appropriate place:

Allium
Anemone blanda
Camassia
Chionodoxa
Colchicum
Crocus
Cyclamen coum; C. hederifolium
Erythronium
Fritillaria meleagris; although F. imperialis will flower
    again it will not necessarily increase in number
Galanthus
Gladiolus byzantinus
Hyacinthoides hispanica; H. non-scripta
Leucojum
Lilium (if well fed)
Muscari (widely available species)
Narcissus
Scilla
Tulipa kaufmanniana (varieties); T. praestans; T. tarda;
    many other species may be reliable if grown at the
    front of a sunny border

As an aside, relying on the worms is behind the 'no-dig' school of thought, which relies on an annual application of mulch (shredded garden waste is ideal), which is broken down over the year and the resulting humus taken down by worms to replenish the soil.

The elimination of perennial weeds and every scrap of their roots is vital, because many can regenerate rapidly from the tiniest section of root that is left in the soil. Whether this is done by digging or through the use of weedkillers is a personal decision, but it has to be said that there are safe weedkillers that will make this a relatively simple task. Those weedkillers based on the chemical glyphosate are particularly safe, being readily biodegradable and harmless to soil life, and they are highly effective at killing the entire root systems of weeds and unwanted grass. Tougher weeds, such as nettles, ground elder and brambles, may be killed safely with a proprietary weedkiller based on ammonium sulphamate, which breaks down to a fertilizer and is thus also harmless to soil life.

SELECTING PLANTS

It makes sense to buy plants from well-established nurseries or garden centres whose reputation depends on selling quality plants. When you buy from a garden centre, there are a number of points to check. If you are buying perennials, make sure that you are actually getting plenty of plant for your money. In spring, before growth has started, it is all too easy to end up with a tiny, weedy shoot. If you are purchasing shrubs and trees in containers, check to see that they are not too old. Woody plants that have been in their pots for a long time tend to be pot bound. The roots trail around and around the inside of the container, which means that they may have problems growing outward again when they are planted out, and this can lead to a permanent lack of stability.

Perhaps the greatest problem with buying plants is incorrect labelling. This is often not the fault of the retailer. It is extraordinarily easy for plants to become wrongly labelled and for mistakes to be carried on from one year to the next. It is worst with bulbs, which should always be bought from a large or reputable speciality dealer, and never from market stalls or even from garden centres if they are sold loose. Even if the retailer hasn't muddled them up, other customers will have done so. Fruit of any kind is a specialist business, for reasons both of plant health and correct naming, and should be bought by mail order from a specialist supplier.

While most garden centres stock a wide range of plants suitable for a mixed border, the selection of perennials and ornamental grasses on offer is rarely as good as the range of shrubs. A better and cheaper selection of perennials is usually carried by specialist nurseries, many of which supply bare-root perennials in autumn and winter by mail order. Many of these specialists exhibit at horticultural shows or similar events, which are usually easier to visit than travelling across country trying to find them personally. Even if you cannot buy what you want on the day, it is possible to see what range of stock they carry so that you can purchase by mail order later.

PLANTING DISTANCES AND NUMBERS

Using a plan to map out the prospective positions for plants will give you a good idea of the numbers you will need, whether there are going to be scattered individuals, groups or loose clumps. But how far apart are they all going to be?

Getting the correct distance between plants in a border is crucial. If they are too far apart, large gaps will be left between plants, leaving bare soil to be dried by the wind and invaded by weeds. If they are too close, extensive thinning or cutting back may be necessary in a year or two so that the border does not look overcrowded and the plants do not begin to compete with each other. The problem is that while perennials grow to a mature size in two to three years, shrubs take much longer.

To get around this problem it may be necessary to indulge in some temporary overplanting. Shrubs

may be planted thickly, with the intention that some will ultimately be taken out; alternatively, the space between them can be filled with perennials, which will be taken out as the shrubs grow. Particularly useful are those short-lived perennials that tend to die out anyway after a few years, especially when they are faced with the competition of expanding shrubs and longer lived perennials. Foxgloves (*Digitalis* species), ox-eye daisies (*Leucanthemum vulgare*) or field mallows (*Malva moschata*) are examples.

Planning for plant spacing is not helped by the vague nature of the information given in many reference books about what is called 'spread'. It is not always specified whether this is ultimate spread or spread after a few years – some perennials can go on spreading to infinity – when what the gardener really wants to know is how quickly a particular plant spreads. As a general rule, allow a space between plants that is about 10 per cent less than the spread usually given for them.

Planting is best done in autumn, except in areas that experience cold and prolonged winters. This is especially important with woody plants, even more so if they are 'bare root' or 'open ground' – that is, they have been dug up from the ground – rather than container grown. Most will make some root growth through winter, which means that they will be in a much better position to face summer drought than if they are planted in spring. Container-grown plants may be planted at any time of year, but this assumes that they will be kept watered if they are planted in midsummer.

When it comes to planting day, you will find that however advanced your plan-making skills, the plan does not accord exactly with reality. There is always

Limited space may mean that the gardener should concentrate on foliage plants with their long season of interest rather than on ephemeral flowers.

something that crops up that necessitates a re-think. It is important that you are open to re-planning at this stage and that your plan does not become something that must be followed to the minutest detail. Bear in mind that some of the world's greatest garden designers do not use plans at all.

Laying out and planting should ideally be done in wet late-autumn or early-winter weather. The great majority of the plants will be dormant, and bare-root perennials can be left lying around on the soil surface for up to week in such weather while you decide where they should go.

PLANTING

Planting is not just a case of popping a plant into a hole in the ground, although on the very best soils this may be all that is needed. Plants will get off to a much better start in life if the soil around them is made more congenial for questing new roots. Consequently, a hole about twice as large as the size of the existing rootball needs to be dug, and the soil that is removed should be broken up. The soil at the bottom of the planting hole should be worked over with a fork to make downwards root penetration easier. This is especially important for shrubs and other woody plants, whose roots will want and need to go downwards. Herbaceous perennials are more interested in sideways movement, so the area around the planting hole should be broken up.

Many container-grown plants will have been growing in a light compost, often based on peat, which makes the transition to garden soil something of a shock, especially if the soil is heavy, and they may simply not make the effort. The roots of new plants will make the transition more easily if they are teased out of the rootball they will have formed around the compost in the pot and the roots spread out in the planting hole.

It has long been the accepted practice to add compost or other organic matter to the soil in the planting hole, along with fertilizer, often phosphorus-rich bonemeal. The latest research indicates that this is not such a good idea because it discourages the roots from spreading to search for nutrients for themselves. Worse still, on poorly drained soils, the water-absorbing organic material may turn the planting hole into a sump, leading to root suffocation and death.

It is true that phosphorus, a vital plant nutrient and essential for healthy root growth, does move extremely slowly through the soil, so if it is to be added it must be dug in before planting and throughout the area of the border, not just the planting holes. There is no need to add phosphorus to soils of normal fertility if only shrubs and perennials are to be grown; it will only encourage the growth of weeds and vigorous grasses

ESTABLISHING PLANTS

Once plants have been introduced to their new surroundings they are vulnerable until they have grown new roots to anchor themselves firmly in place and to obtain all the nutrients and moisture they need. A helping hand at this stage can mean the difference between life and death and certainly affect the speed with which plants reward you with growth and flowers.

Watering

If plants are planted in autumn they should have enough moisture for their immediate needs, although an exceptionally dry autumn and winter might make some additional irrigation necessary. Particularly vulnerable are evergreens, especially in drying winds, and they can be protected in such weather by being covered in sacking, which can then

Border maintenance

The following table outlines the basics of border maintenance throughout the year. If reducing maintenance to a minimum is important, look at it in conjunction with pages 154–6.

TYPE OF PLANT	LATE WINTER/ EARLY SPRING	SPRING	SUMMER	AUTUMN/ EARLY WINTER
General	Dig out perennials weeds; put mulch in place; apply rotted compost and manure and dig in fertilizer if used	Remove or treat early emerging weeds	Irrigate if necessary, especially new plants and annuals; remove weeds as they appear	General tidying up and cutting back of unwanted growth; spread rotted compost and manure; dig in fertilizer
Shrubs/small trees	Prune roses if necessary	Prune early-flowering shrubs after flowering to restrict size if necessary		
Dwarf shrubs		Cut back winter-flowering heathers	Cut back lavenders and summer-flowering heathers	Cut back late-flowering heathers
Climbers	Prune large-flowered clematis	Prune early-flowering varieties after flowering to restrict size if necessary		
Perennials	Cut back dead growth if not already done	Put supports in place for tall species likely to fall over; protect new growth from slugs	Tie floppy varieties to supports; cut off dead flowers or untidy growth if necessary	Cut back dead growth if wished; otherwise leave until later in the winter
Bulbs		Remove dead, not living, foliage		Time for planting; the earlier the better
Hardy annuals	Prepare sites for sowing by digging over and raking soil	Sow outside in prepared soil		Remove and compost dead plants; make some autumn sowings for early summer flower
Half-hardy annuals/bedding	Make first sowings under glass or indoors	Plant outside once danger of frosts has passed		Remove and compost dead plants after first frosts
Seasonal half-hardy plants	Start to feed plants indoors as light gets stronger	Plant outside once danger of frosts has passed	Dig up, pot up and take indoors before first frosts; cut back if necessary; dry off tuberous roots (e.g., dahlias, gladioli and cannas)	Overwinter plants in a light place; water sparingly; store tubers in dark, dry, cool but frost-free place, checking occasionally

be sprayed with water to reduce moisture loss from the leaves. A hi-tech alternative is to spray them with an anti-desiccation compound, which temporarily coats the leaves with a layer that reduces water loss.

During periods of dry summer weather additional watering may be needed in the first year. This will be almost inevitable for plants that have been planted in spring rather than in autumn or early winter. Particularly vulnerable will be anything that

ABOVE: The easiest way to support plants is with ready-made structures that can be placed over them in spring.

RIGHT: Perennials vary greatly in their staking requirements; delphiniums, for example, almost always need support, but many other species do not.

has been planted bare root rather than from a container. Plants should be encouraged to send down roots to reach their own moisture rather than to grow surface roots that depend on irrigation. This is why it is usually best to water only when it becomes absolutely necessary, and then irrigation needs to soak the ground – a light sprinkling that wets only the top few centimetres is no good. The best way to water is often to let a hose run water over the ground so that it can soak in rather than using a sprinkler. Mulches (see page 150) applied over damp ground help enormously to reduce water loss.

Weeding

Weeds compete with newly planted and vulnerable plants for nutrients, light and moisture. They must be kept at bay in the new border even more than in an established one. Perennial weeds that sprout from bits of buried root should have been removed while the site was being prepared, but if some regenerate they can be dug out or treated with the weedkillers mentioned on page 141. A weedkiller is often useful in borders where it may be difficult or undesirable to disturb the soil and is also particularly useful where a layer of mulch on the soil surface makes digging out weeds difficult.

Weeds, mostly annual ones, that germinate from seed on the soil surface may be easily hoed off, which is best done when they are small. If hoeing is done in windy or dry weather such seedlings will die rapidly if they are left on the soil surface.

The dying days of the year can be a magical time in the garden, with dew and low light illuminating grasses and the seedheads of perennials. A variety of aster provides the last flowers of the season.

Applying a Mulch

The germination of weed seeds can be drastically reduced if the soil is covered with a mulch, which will also greatly reduce water loss. The most often seen types of mulch are made from chipped bark or waste wood and are easily obtained. Unlike some other mulching materials, such as straw or various waste agricultural products, chipped bark does not blow around and does not look unattractive. It must not be dug into the soil during weeding or planting, however, because this reduces its effectiveness and can cause nitrogen depletion of the soil as it decays. For this reason all planting of the border must be complete before a mulch is applied.

Loose mulches like chipped bark do not stop perennial weed roots breaking through. If this is likely to be a problem it might be worth considering using the kind of plastic sheeting often used in commercial landscaping operations. This is expensive in large quantities and environmentally unfriendly, but it is highly effective. It needs to be laid before planting and holes cut into it for planting. It will also need covering with bark mulch to provide an attractive finish.

BORDER MAINTENANCE
Staking

One of the time-consuming tasks associated with the traditional herbaceous border was the staking and tying in of tall, top-heavy perennials. Modern staking devices have reduced a lot of the work involved, and if you want to avoid having any to do, choose varieties that do not need staking. Many garden centres sell various wire supports, most of which need to be placed around or over the growing plants in spring so that the new shoots grow through the supports.

Dead-heading and Cutting Back

Many gardeners dead-head flowers once they have finished. This certainly improves the appearance of the border, especially with those plants — certain roses or camellias, for example — that do not drop their dead flowerheads. It can also stimulate the production of more flowers or a second flowering. Where there are a lot of dead flowers and stems to remove, it is more easily done with shears than individually, the flower stems being cut at the base.

Late-summer- and autumn-flowering perennials will not flower again, and cutting back is simply one part of the annual round of clearing up dead growth. Leaving dead stems for most of winter is a possibility: they can look wonderful in hoar frost or snow, and birds will benefit from being able to eat the seeds and any insect life that is lurking in the old flowerheads.

Pruning and Training

Pruning and training are relevant only to shrubs in the border. Generally, we want newly planted shrubs and small trees to grow as fast as possible, which leaves pruning to be a concern for later rather than earlier years. There are, however, a few plants that pruning can encourage to flower more quickly — wisteria, for example — or more profusely — modern roses, for example — or it may be necessary to establish a particular shape, as in topiary. Pruning is always something of a specialized activity, with each species having its own peculiarities. There are several good reference books on pruning that can be consulted.

Propagation

Large mixed borders or the open border style require large numbers of perennials, which can be prohibitively expensive to buy. Propagation is a vast and

Dividing herbaceous perennials

Examples are shown of herbaceous perennials that can be divided into smaller, independent pieces. Plants may be torn apart by hand or pulled apart by inserting two forks and levering them apart. Because cutting involves going across the natural tear lines of roots, it should be carried out if there is no other way of separating the pieces.

Carex

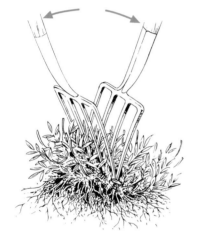

Stachys lanata

Hosta

Aster

complex subject, yet there are several means of increasing plants that are simple and invaluable for the gardener who wants to avoid spending a fortune at the garden centre.

Most perennials can be divided when they are dormant, although ornamental grasses should be divided only when they are actively growing, which generally means late spring. Any little piece that has both some root and shoot will grow and can be treated as a new plant, although in practice the smaller divisions should not be planted out in situations where conditions are less than perfect. Instead, they can be grown on for a year in a nursery bed before they are put into their permanent positions.

Old established perennial clumps can be incredibly hard and woody, and can be divided only with a certain amount of skill and a lot of effort. It is worth it, however, for they can yield a large number of new shoots, which will grow vigorously when they are separated and planted out.

Adapting an Existing Border

Many people are faced with an existing border rather than a clean slate. It may be a border in an obviously parlous state or it may just be dull, in need of a bit of spicing up with some more interesting plants. If it is a border in the garden of a property you have just bought it is a good idea not to do too much right away; leave it for the best part of a season to see what bulbs come up in spring and what perennials emerge and to see how much shade trees cast in summer. And what weeds there are, too!

The following are common problems in old borders, together with some suggestions for dealing with them:

• Perennial weeds growing among worthwhile plants. Digging out perennial weeds can be immensely time consuming and often, if they are growing intimately with garden plants, ineffective. Certain herbicides, notably the glyphosate-based ones and the ammonium sulphamate crystals mentioned on page 141, can be used among plants that you want to keep. They will spread through the system of whatever they are sprayed on, but will not spread through the soil into neighbouring plants. If weeds are intimately bound up with desirable plants it is possible to use a mixture of wallpaper paste and weedkiller for accurate treatment, painting it on to the weeds with a brush.

• Overhanging trees creating large areas of shade. Lower branches can often be removed with little effect on the overall appearance of the tree, but with a great increase in the amount of light reaching the ground.

• Old shrubs taking up space. Elderly shrubs can assume monstrous proportions, with vast quantities of old branches making an unattractive thicket. Such plants can usually be cut back and growth thinned by the removal of stems. A more extreme solution is to cut the plant right back to ground level. Most will successfully rejuvenate themselves with lots of healthy new growth.

If you feel that there are too many shrubs it may be necessary to remove some. This is not a task to be undertaken lightly. Unlike trees, which can be cleanly cut down and the stump killed if it is not removed, old shrubs have a multiplicity of branches and often form wide bases that take up too much space to be left in the ground. Their removal, by digging and cutting through the roots, can seem a veritable labour of Hercules.

Remember that it is inadvisable to try to grow a new shrub or tree on the site of an older plant of the same kind.

• Old perennials taking up space. Overgrown clumps of goldenrod (*Solidago* species) and Michaelmas daisies (*Aster novi-belgii* varieties) are the most usually encountered perennials, along with mats of geraniums and huge woody clumps of irises. These can be dug up and divided, with a proportion replanted and the rest given away (old borders often have enough to supply several charity plant stalls) or even discarded. This can be done at any time when the plants are dormant. The same is true of big old clusters of bulbs, which are best split and redistributed in early summer or midsummer, before their roots have started to grow. Once they have been split, you will find perennials and bulbs putting on a lot of healthy new growth.

Consider carefully what features of an old border are worth retaining or making a special feature of. The following are some of the possibilities:

• Mature shrubs may be a nuisance but they may have potential. Anything that is slow growing, like an azalea or some viburnums, will be practically irreplaceable, so if it is fine specimen consider making it the centrepiece of the redesigned border, with other plants chosen to complement it. Early-spring-flowering shrubs are especially welcome; even an overgrown forsythia may be worth saving by cutting back hard.

• Clipped shrubs that have been allowed to grow loose. Yews, box and *Lonicera nitida* are frequently planted for edging or topiary-style clipped shapes and then neglected. They can be cut back hard, well into old wood, and they will send out new growth, especially if they are fed well. After a year or two the process of shaping them to your design can begin.

• Dwarf conifers that have been around for so long they are no longer dwarf. These are grossly overplanted in my opinion, yet if there is a fine specimen, particularly one of the upright ones, it is worth keeping. Good vertical growing shapes are few and far between. Others can be removed without too much trouble and make good firewood.

• Mature climbers, like a honeysuckle or *Clematis montana* that has been allowed to run riot, can be monsters to deal with, yet it would take years for you to grow one to the same size. The same is especially true of old vines and wisteria, and these are worth any effort to save. Old climbers need to be cut back where they interfere with other plants or your future plans or where they threaten to crush whatever structure supports them, but they can be left alone if they look as if they are doing no harm. It is worth inspecting their supports and erecting a framework of stout poles to help carry their weight if the originals look weak.

When you are adapting an old border, the following is a useful list of questions you need to ask yourself:

• What is the border lacking?
  – colour and interest at a particular season
  – a clear colour scheme
  – attractive foliage
  – strong plant shapes
  – a focal point, which could be provided by a plant or an artefact
  – a sense of unity; perhaps there are too many disparate elements
  – plants to give a sense of height
  – too many upright growers, without lower growing clump formers to balance them
• Is it the right size and shape?
  – can it be enlarged (or even reduced); many borders are too narrow to fit in many plants or develop much depth
  – if it is a boring, straight strip, is it possible to introduce some curves to add interest, in

particular so that the whole thing is not seen all at once

- Are there any particular plants that you would like to grow?
  - are they compatible (in terms of conditions needed and looks) with what is there already

LOW-MAINTENANCE BORDERS

While many people love their gardens, there are also many who wish that they were not such hard work. Unfortunately, the truth is that the best gardens are the ones that have plenty of time and attention lavished on them. And, it has to be said, the mixed border is not the most labour-saving of garden forms. Nevertheless, gardens and borders less demanding of time can be attractive, if the right plants are chosen. It is plant selection that is crucial in minimizing the amount, not only of time, but also of money, water and other inputs, that go into

gardens. Minimizing maintenance is all about doing as little watering, feeding, pruning, weeding and pest and disease control as possible, so we need to find plants that can look after themselves.

As we have seen, using only permanent hardy plants, which will remain in the same place year after year, is a huge step in the direction of the low-maintenance border. Time-consuming annuals and bedding add an undeniable splash, but they are really only the icing on the cake.

Watering and Feeding

Watering and feeding can be reduced to practically nothing if plants are chosen that are suited to the conditions of the site — that is, that can flourish with the water and nutrients naturally available. This is why the selection of plants suited to the conditions of your garden is so important. A reference book that includes detailed information about each plant's

Low-maintenance perennials

The following perennials do not need staking or cutting back during the growing season;
they will reliably build up into good clumps.

	HEIGHT × SPREAD	FLOWERS AND FOLIAGE	NOTES
Aquilegia vulgaris	1 × 0.3m/3 × 1ft	Flowers in pinks and blue-mauves in early summer	Self-seeds; tolerant; will grow in light shade
Campanula persicifolia	40 × 60cm/16 × 24in	Blue bells above mats of glossy foliage in early summer	Tolerant; will grow in shade
Echinops ritro	1.2 × 1.2m/4 × 4ft	Blue, globe-shaped flowerhead above divided leaves in midsummer	Does best in sun
Geranium × magnificum	60 × 50cm/24 × 20in	Mauve flowers in early summer; dark foliage	Grows in sun or shade
Rudbeckia 'Juligold'	1.5 × 0.7m/5ft × 2ft 4in	Yellow daisies on tall stems in late summer	Vigorous; needs sun
Veronicastrum virginicum	1.2 × 0.5m/4ft × 1ft 8in	Upright stems with spikes of pale mauve flowers in mid- to late summer	Needs sun

cultural requirements combined with an understanding of your garden conditions are invaluable when it comes to choosing species.

To some extent, water can be saved by applying a layer of mulch – chipped bark or other similar material – on the soil surface, and this will also reduce weed growth. Planting through mulch is not as straightforward as planting into soil, because it is vital not to mix mulch and soil if the mulch is to work, so a mulch is practicable only when it is used with permanent plants in borders rather than with annuals and other temporary plants.

Pruning and Training

Pruning and cutting back can be reduced if plants are chosen that are the right size for their position and have a tidy habit of growth. This is especially important when mixed borders are being planted because space is usually at a premium, and large, spreading or invasive plants can quickly smother their smaller or less vigorous neighbours in the planting scheme. Making sure that a plant will physically fit into your border is vital if the regular cutting back of lunging stems or digging out of creeping rootstocks is to be avoided.

Some plants, such as modern hybrid tea roses, need regular – that is, annual – pruning for successful growth. Yet others, such as old-fashioned and species roses, do not and are happy if they are pruned every few years. Before committing yourself to making such plants a major feature of your border, it makes obvious sense to find out the group in which your chosen varieties belong.

The majority of shrubs, small trees and climbers that are sold today do not need fancy pruning to make them perform. However, pruning can sometimes increase the amount of flower you get – this is true of clematis hybrids, for instance – or it can

sometimes result in flowering on younger plants. If it is left to itself, for example, wisteria might take many years to produce flowers.

The main reason for pruning shrubs in mixed borders is to restrict their size (which would not be such a problem if the right ones were chosen in the first place). If this is the reason, a general rule is that they should be pruned immediately after flowering; if pruning is left until autumn, the following year's flowers may be drastically reduced.

We all have a tendency (including many professionals) to overplant, putting plants too close together. This is natural because it means that we get results more quickly. The price we pay, though, is that the years to come will involve more work: cutting back shrubs that are growing into each other, dividing clumps of perennials and maybe even removing some plants altogether. If reducing

---

Plants to avoid in low-maintenance borders

The following perennials generally need staking, get eaten by slugs or are short lived:

Alcea (hollyhock)
Anthemis tinctoria (varieties)
Aster novi-belgii (hybrids)
Cheiranthus and *Erysimum* (wallflowers)
Chrysanthemum
Delphinium
Dianthus (except smaller varieties)
Gaillardia
Hosta
Lupinus
Malva
Penstemon
Phlox (hybrids)
Rosa (hybrid teas and modern floribundas)
and anything that is not totally hardy in your area.

labour is important, you should be careful not to overplant in the first place. Gaps can always be filled temporarily with annuals in the first year or two.

Putting plants together that are equally balanced will also help to reduce the amount of cutting back and dividing. It makes sense not to mix anything described as 'invasive' with slower growing plants. As a general rule plants from similar habitats often grow at a similar pace; moisture-loving plants tend to grow big fast, even when they are in soils that are not especially wet, whereas those from difficult environments, such as shade or dry areas, are slower growing and easily swamped by more vigorous plants, even if conditions are better than those they are used to.

Pests and Diseases

Many gardeners spend a great deal of time and money trying to cope, often unsuccessfully, with the natural enemies of plants, the pests and diseases that infect, infest and disfigure them. Healthy plants suffer much less than those under stress, which is yet another reason for choosing plants that will grow well naturally in your garden. Growing roses, for example, on a thin, dry soil will only result in poor growth and more fungal diseases.

The great thing about a well-planned mixed border is that it contains a rich diversity of plant life. Pests and diseases thrive on unnaturally dense populations of one plant, so growing a lot of roses in one border together with little else is asking for trouble – the bugs can hop from plant to plant in no time. What is more, a really good mixture of different plants means that you are, in effect, hedging your bets – if a plant gets a disease one year and looks awful, the chances are that its neighbours will look fine and disguise it.

Learning to live with pests and diseases is part of

the solution. Few are fatal to plants and most are only a short-lived nuisance. Striving for the perfect garden, utterly without blemishes, is a recipe for hard work.

Low-maintenance Perennials

Shrubs have been a major feature of low-maintenance planting for many years now, as they have always been regarded as requiring less maintenance than perennials, which, at the least, require an annual clearing away of dead stems at the end of the season. Perennials were always seen as needing more care: feeding and regular division to make them grow, and staking to stop them falling over when they did grow. Modern thinking on perennials has changed. There are now far more varieties available that do not need the level of maintenance of the older varieties, and ideas on how they should be looked after have changed, too. Many of the 'modern' perennials are either natural species or are close to their wild ancestors, plants that are usually tougher and less demanding than the highly bred hybrids.

Perennials in old-fashioned herbaceous borders were usually fed generously – too generously, in fact – so they grew top heavy. Not feeding may result in smaller plants, but those plants are more likely to stand up without support. After all, wildflowers are usually able to stand up without staking, aren't they?

To a large extent our perception of the use of perennials in the garden has changed, and we are now more likely to regard them as low-maintenance plants. We no longer expect to see neatly delineated clumps of delphiniums and chrysanthemums standing as if on parade. The cottage garden and the wildflower gardening movements have made us accept that these plants can be grown in a more carefree and relaxed way.

FURTHER READING

Anything by Christopher Lloyd, Beth Chatto or Graham Stuart Thomas is worth reading. They are all consummate plantspeople, whose ideas have shaped much of what is best in the modern British border (and much beyond these isles, too). In particular, Graham Stuart Thomas' *Perennial Garden Plants* (Dent, London, 1990) is a wonderful reference book of particular value to those planting borders.

The most valuable reference books are the two Royal Horticultural Society encyclopedias, edited by Christopher Brickell. The earlier *The RHS Gardeners' Encyclopedia of Plants and Flowers* (Dorling Kindersley, London, 1989) may have its drawbacks as a reference book, but it is a dream for anyone designing a border. The two volumes of *Perennials* by Roger Phillips and Rix

(Pan, London, 1991) are also useful as reference books.

Grasses are unfortunately not well covered by books, but *Gardening with Grasses* by Piet Oudolf and Michael King (Frances Lincoln, London, 1998) is extremely useful, full of good ideas, as will be anything else that Piet Oudolf gets to publish.

Of books specifically on borders *Best Borders* by Tony Lord (Frances Lincoln, London, 1994) is much the best, concentrating on the classic British borders. Andrew Lawson's *The Gardener's Book of Colour* (Frances Lincoln, London, 1996) is far and away the best book on this central topic, while my own *The New Perennial Garden* (Frances Lincoln, London, 1996) is the only available English-language work on the more naturalistic 'open borders' of Germany and Holland.

ACKNOWLEDGEMENTS

This book is inevitably influenced by gardens with great borders. National Trust properties generally have the best classic ones. Among more modern or smaller scale example, Hadspen House, Castle Cary, Somerset, gardened by Norri and Sandra Pope, reveals a deployment of colour that is as about as skilled as you will find anywhere. Christopher Lloyd's garden at Great Dixter in East Sussex is another masterpiece, but with more emphasis on contrast than harmony. Wollerton Old Hall, Shropshire, open under the National Garden Scheme and created by Lesley Jenkins, is a personal favourite, with accessible ideas for smaller gardens. Piet Oudolf's borders, mostly in the Netherlands, are among the best being created at the moment, and the garden and nursery run by Piet and his wife Anja at Hummelo, near Arnhem, is an absolute must. For the contemporary open border, which has evolved in Germany, the most intimate example and thus most relevant to smaller gardens, is Hermanshoff in Weinheim, which was created by Urs Walser.

PICTURE CREDITS

Anne Hyde 17 (Fieldhead, Yorks), 23 (Lakemount, Cork, Eire), 28 (Fieldhead, Yorks), 120 (Home Farm, Balscote, Oxon); **Noël Kingsbury** 106–7, 127–8 (Hermanshof. Designer: Urs Walser); **Andrew Lawson** 2 (The Menagerie, Northamptonshire), 4 (Brooklands, Dumfries & Galloway), 6–7 (Old Rectory, Burghfield), 8 (Designer: Wendy Launderdale), 10 (NT for Scotland, Inverewe), 12 (Manor House, Bledlow, Bucks), 16 (Sticky Wicket, Buckland Newton, Dorset), 18–9 (Designer: Wendy Launderdale), 21 (Lawhead Croft, Tarbrax, Quantoxhead, Somerset), 31 (Designer: Wendy Lauderdale), 35 (Court House, East Quantoxhead, Somerset), 44 (Gothic House, Charlebury, Oxon), 48 (Shuckletts, Ramsden, Oxon), 57 (Gothic House, Charlbury, Oxon), 59 (Gothic House, Charlebury, Oxon), 66 (NT, Powis Castle), 73 (Wollerton Old Hall, Shropshire), 84 (Wollerton Old Hall, Shropshire), 86 (Gothic House, Charlbury, Oxon), 87 (Brooklands, Dumfries & Galloway), 95 (Old Chapel, Chalford, Glos), 96 (Coton Manor, Northants), 112 (NT, Tintinhull, Somerset), 131 (Ethne Clarke, Norfolk), 138 (Flinton Hall, Notts), 143 (Designer: Wendy Lauderdale), 146(L) (Brook Cottage, Alkerton, Oxon); **Anthony Lord** 5(L) (Arley Hall, Cheshire), 9 (Arley Hall, Cheshire), 11 (Arley Hall, Cheshire), 15 (Killesburg, Stuttgart, Germany), 25, 37 (The Manor House, Heslington, nr. York), 39 (NT, Packwood House, Warwickshire), 42 (Barnsley House, nr. Cirencester, Glos), 45 (Barnsley, nr. Cirencester, Glos), 51, 53 (NT, Packwood House, Warwickshire), 55 (T) (The Manor House, Heslington, nr. York), 55(B) Landgartenschau (1996), Böblingen, Germany), 3, 65, 67, 74–5 (The Manor House, Heslington, nr. York), 79, 81 (Arley Hall, Cheshire), 88 (Great Dixter, Northiam, East Sussex), 93, 94, 97 (Great Dixter, Northiam, East Sussex), 107 (Arley Hall, Cheshire), 108–9 (NT, Hardwick Hall, Derbyshire), 110 (Broughton Castle, nr. Banbury), 111, 113 (Great Dixter, Northiam, East Sussex), 115 (Landgartenschau (1996), Böblingen, Germany), 116–7 (Barnsley House, nr. Cirencester, Glos), 119, 121–2, 123 (Barnsley House, nr. Cirencester, Glos), 132 (Landgartenschau (1996), Böblingen, Germany) 135, 136 (Denmans, West Sussex); **Clive Nichols** 1 (White Windows, Hampshire), 5 (R) (Arley), 68 (Old Rectory, Burghfield), 98–9 (Chenies Manor, Bucks), 146–7 (Arley); **Piet Oudolf** 139, 148–9.

INDEX

Page numbers in *italic* refer to the illustrations

exposed sites 33

Fatsia japonica 86
fences 24, 27
fennel *42*, 79, 91
ferns 28, 30, 33, 89, 91, 92
fertilizers 144
Festuca glauca 45
filler plants 42, *43*, 46
foliage: aromatic 50; colour 98–102;
   evergreens 92; 'hot' borders 109;
   repetition and rhythm 49; shapes
   86–9, *87*, *88*, *90–1*; shrubs 119;
   silver *106–7*, 112, 114; small
   gardens 28; texture 91, *93*; theme
   plants 45
formal gardens 23
formal plant shapes 80, 81
Forsythia 42, 44, 153; *F. × intermedia*
   'Spectabilis' 105
foxgloves 47, 76, *110*, *135*, 142
Fremontodendron californicum 105
French marigolds 50
Fritillaria imperialis 129; *F. meleagris* 129
frost *32*, 33
fruit 137–8, *137*, *138*
fuchsias 91

Galanthus nivalis 43, 62
Gallium odoratum 43, *43*
Genista aetnensis 80
Geranium 43, *43*, 64–5, *74–5*, 112, 153;
   G. endressii 53, 125; *G.* 'Johnson's
   Blue' 63; *G. × magnificum 18–19*,
   107, 154; *G. × oxonianum* 125; *G. ×
   oxonianum* 'Wargrave Pink' 110; *G.
   psilostemon* 108; *G. wallichianum*
   'Buxton's Variety' 109
gladioli 137
goldenrod 153
grasses 126, *127*; coastal gardens 34;
   division 152; evergreens 92; shady
   gardens 30; shape 84; soils 35, 37,
   38; theme plants 45; windy
   gardens 33
gravel gardens 16, 35
grey foliage *106–7*
Griselinia littoralis 80, 81
ground-cover plants 47
grouping plants 47, 49–53, *52*, *56*
Gunnera manicata 89; *G. tinctoria 87*

hart's tongue fern 91
hazel, corkscrew 80, 84
heathers 38, 45, 50, 72, 118, 121

Hebe 34, 45; *H. cupressoides* 'Boughton
   Dome' 93; *H.* 'Midsummer
   Beauty' 118; *H.* 'White Gem' 103
Hedera 27; *H. helix* 'Gold Heart' 130
hedges 24, *26*, 27
height 76–9, *77*, *78*
Helichrysum italicum 50
Heliotropium arborescens 49
Helleborus 28, 122; *H. orientalis* 124
Hemerocallis 66, *123*; *H.* 'Golden
   Chimes' 125
herbs 137, 138
heuchera *122*
honeysuckle *10*, 27, *48*, 153
Hosta 18–19, 33; *H. sieboldiana 31*, *87*
'hot' borders 107–9
Hyacinthoides non-scripta 102
Hydrangea sargentiana 93

Ilex × altaclerensis 'Golden King' 119
informal gardens 23
informal plant shapes 80, 81–4
Iris 112, 153; *I. sibirica* 35, 125
island beds 7, 10–14, *14*, 133
ivies 27, 33

jasmine 91
Juniperus 80; *J. scopulorum* 'Skyrocket'
   76

Knautia macedonica 63
Kniphofia 21, 53, 84
Kolkwitzia amabilis 63

Lamium 43, *43*; *L. maculatum* 124; *L.m.*
   'Beacon Silver' 114
laurels 80
Laurus nobilis 119
Lavandula (lavender) *26*, 28, 35, 40, 91,
   112, 118, 121; *L. angustifolia*
   'Hidcote' 109; *L. stoechas*
   'Pedunculata' 50
Lavatera 'Rosea' 63
lawns 20, 35
leaves *see* foliage
Leucanthemella serotina 6–7, 125
Leucanthemum vulgare 142
Levisticum officinalis 138
liatris *51*
Libertia grandiflora 103
ligularia 66
Lilium regale 129
Limnanthes douglasii 133
Lonicera 27; *L. nitida* 153; *L. periclymenum*
   'Graham Thomas' 130

lovage 138
low-maintenance borders 154–6
lupins 12, *74–5*
Lychnis coronaria 108
Lythrum salicaria 108; *L. virgatum* 108

Macleaya cordata 25
magenta flowers 108, 112–14
Magnolia grandiflora 93; *M. stellata* 62
Mahonia 'Charity' 119
maintenance 145, 150–2
mallows 142
Malus 134; *M. tschonoskii* 134
Malva moschata 110, 142
maples 134
marguerites 136–7
Matteucia struthiopteris 63
Matthiola 49
Melianthus major 86
Mentha × piperita 'Citrata' 50
Michaelmas daisies 6–7, 36, 43, 65,
   153
micro-climates 33
Milium effusum 'Aureum' 126
mimulus 24
Miscanthus sinensis 126
moist soils 40
Monarda 65; *M.* 'Cambridge Scarlet'
   96; *M.* 'Capricorn' 109
mulches 141, 148, 150, 155
Musa basjoo 86
Muscari aucheri 129
Myrtus communis 50

Narcissus 43, *43*, 64, *128*; *N.* 'Actaea'
   129; *N.* 'February Gold' 129
nasturtiums 104
nicotiana 113
Nigella 112; *N. damascena* 'Persian
   Jewels' 133

obelisks 93, 130
Omphalodes cappadocica 105; *O. linifolia
   98–9*
open borders 14–16, *15–16*, 23, 79
organic matter 140–1, 144
ox-eye daisies 142

palms 34, 136
Papaver orientale 47, 59, *74–5*; *P.
   somniferum* 133
Parthenocissus 27; *P. quinquefolia* 130
pastel borders 109–14
patio plants 72, 136–7
Paulownia tomentosa 86